Bet the Farm!

Be More Prepared Today to Reach Your Dreams!
Unleash the Productivity within You

Antwain Tate Goode, PhD

BET THE FARM!
Be More Prepared Today to Reach Your Dreams!
Unleash the Productivity within You

iUniverse books may be ordered through booksellers or by contacting:

iUniverse
1663 Liberty Drive
Bloomington, IN 47403
www.iuniverse.com
1-800-Authors (1-800-288-4677)

ISBN: 978-1-4917-7092-4 (sc)
ISBN: 978-1-4917-7180-8 (hc)
ISBN: 978-1-4917-7179-2 (e)

Library of Congress Control Number: 2015910616

Print information available on the last page.

iUniverse rev. date: 07/22/2015

Table of Contents

- ➤ Pressure!
- ➤ Rehearse, Refine, Polish and Deliver.
- ➤ Decisions, decisions.
- ➤ Apply your resources. Get some help!
- ➤ Remember: no regrets! Your dreams are at your grasp.

Dedication

To my wife Andrea,

Thank you for supporting my dreams of building a stronger bridge for our family. We have together sailed to uncharted areas of the mind and touched the lives of many. May this book provide a framework for my children (Kennedy & Harrison) to risk it all when the time comes!

To my mother Marva M. Goode,

Your "Tenacious" spirit has pushed me to confidently give hope to cultures everywhere. Your labors of love were not in vain and your passion to never quit drives me to excellence!

A heartfelt note to Dr. Alberta Haynes Herron, Retired Associate Vice President for Institutional Effectiveness and Founding Dean of the Norcross Graduate School, High Point University

Your insight, confidence, and willingness to share have opened up new corridors of my mind. You have shown me the way through education and now I can soar with the eagles! Your passion to forge excellence in others works! And I got the memo....

The excitement will build as you read *Bet the Farm*. My book is written for the sole purpose of unleashing productivity within people. The ideas presented will supercharge people to deliver top performances in organizations and to reinvigorate people to help others around the world. The topics covered and solutions offered will spur creative thought and can be fused with organizational objectives to help you meet professional and personal goals.

The experience gained while working in the industrial distribution business sector—over 24 years in operations management, supply chain management, strategic sales development, and customer service—enabled me to forge incredible relationships with incredible organizations. Many leaders have helped me develop my skills along the way. These skills drove customer-first solutions across multiple vertical markets, including identifying and implementing process improvements, project management solutions, team collaboration projects, and resource allocation initiatives that enhance organizational profitability. My experience and record of achievement for developing customer-first solutions for many Fortune 500 manufacturing organizations such as RJR Tobacco, Weyerhaeuser, Vulcan Materials, K & W Cafeterias, Johnson Controls, Allied Signal, BMW, EI Dupont, Intermech, CBRE, TW Garner, Rock Tenn, Kaba Ilco, and Wayne Farms have provided a wealth of creative and productive solutions.

Working in the industrial distribution industry has provided me incredible insight, and a training ground for me to develop community relationships, strategic planning, and performance improvement strategies. An intense focus on community relationships has allowed me to share diverse perspectives on leadership. Partnering with the North Carolina Chamber of Commerce and Rotary Club professional organizations allowed me to meet incredible leaders and formulate private sector relationships to serve the Winston-Salem community. Organizations today want and need people who can make a difference and spark innovation.

You also have what it takes to deliver the perfect employer/employee or seller/client "Knock out Punch!" We have unlimited mental resources that are untapped and ready to go. People around the world wrestle every day to find that thing, that person, that opportunity that will magically turn everything around. The Lord has truly opened up my spirit and my mind. He has allowed me to use my energy, attitude, passion and power to ignite others. You have greatness that will be exposed as you read, write and follow the instructions in my book. Absorb the chapters and let the techniques, tips, charts, "aha" moments, and customer quotes build your confidence. Unleashing your creativity will activate the needed momentum to make your productivity go. Whether you are a new professional who does not know where to begin or a tenured professional who needs to tool up, my book will reinforce all of the positive attributes that you have and create new ones. You will receive the most prized possession, the magical pot of gold: "Client Loyalty".

The stars have aligned, you are more prepared today, and the time is now! Bet The Farm!

Go for it all…

Antwain Tate Goode, PhD

Acknowledgements

This section is dedicated to a special group of individuals who gave me a chance, who pushed me to believe in my skill sets, and who helped unlock my productivity. To begin with, the following clients deserve recognition for helping me develop thick skin: Ron Willard, Tommy Hickman, Jeff Watts, Larry Mccan, and George Pilcher. Throughout each character building session with these leaders new layers of confidence were created. The next clients taught me to have a heightened awareness and sincerity in regard to quality: Neal Hackworth, Ken Cox, Barry Cleary, Rick Edwards, Landon Hicks, and Kenneth Gordon; I cannot thank you enough for emphasizing that quality lasts, quality holds value and quality people should be held onto!

The clients who provided the best example of how to develop a supporting cast are the leaders of K & W Cafeteria. Thank you Dee Rowland, Dax Allred, Bill Allred, Todd Smith, Ahwanda Jamison, and Jimmy Sizemore for helping me see the power of family in a new light. Your letter of recommendation for me to enter High Point University's Norcross Graduate School was a key milestone in my development. You have taught me that love can be felt through an organization, as you have many employees who remain faithful after 40 or 50 years! Yes you have the recipe for delivering great food and inviting people like me to share in your family's success.

The client who helped me to build, strengthen, and anchor my presentational skills are the leaders of Vulcan Materials. Pete Roberts, Randy Puckett, Fred Mchugh, Chris Ashley, Carrie Myers, Travis Hodge, Dan Lawless, and Danny Taylor, thank you for allowing me to present at your 7:00 am safety meetings. Your relentless focus on employee safety stretched my presentational abilities in many ways. Sharing authentic perspectives on talent development helped me to RRPD (Rehearse, Refine, Polish, and Deliver) on all presentations!

Finally, a special thank you to a new client who pushed my creative energies forward: Dan Thompson of Johnson Controls. Your insight in the art of problem solving is outstanding. Your leadership challenged me to become more innovative and relentless to help people find new global solutions. It is because of your faith in my tenacity that I will always work to own the collaborative elements of innovation.

The freedom that America offers gives us incredible opportunities every day to attain high aspirations. I have been so fortunate over the years to have met incredible leaders who have shaped my life. My workplace managers have all been stellar in grooming me. James Johnson, Dale Shoop, Al Nantz, Mike Roberts, Tom Massari, and Jeff Wayne, represent the greatest battleships of leadership in my life and I am humbly thankful for working under them. A special note is needed for friends Kevin Earley, Tamera Fox, Jay Straughan, Steven Robertson, Justin Ricketts, Christopher Jensen, Dr. Tiffanie Nichols, and Pastor Ed Smith for pushing me to be a better leader in manufacturing consulting. The ability to understand value, corporate initiatives, and expectations have helped me synthesize many business perspectives from around the world.

The secret weapon which unlocked the many corridors of my mind and enabled me to organize my thoughts to write this book came from the collective confidence of my graduate professors at the High Point University Norcross Graduate School in High Point, North Carolina. Under the leadership of the president Dr. Nido Qubein, High Point University has been the family that has developed my scholarly skill set. First, Dr. Alberta H. Herron: thank you for the tough love and the many one-on-one character building sessions. Dr. Herron, your mentorship, eagle eyed vision, and tenacity was the lighthouse that guided my path in this book. There are people in your life that you need to meet and people who need to meet you! Fortunately for me, the Lord placed in my path an incredible leader and editor Ms. Leanne Jernigan. Your relentless literary expertise, patience, guidance and support helped me to deliver my thoughts. High Point University has so many talented individuals and you are one of its brightest stars!

Dr. James Wehrley, Dr. Anne Grube, and Dr. Stephanie Crofton your perspectives on scholarly leadership have pushed me to link high-level business practice and business theory in the classroom. Dr. A. Berry Crawford, former Culp Chair of Ethics: thank you for pushing me to seek truth in every endeavor. The chapters in this book are straight from the heart and the life lessons that you put into your lectures anchored my focus. Dr. Richard D. Parker: thank you for your lectures on the awesome power of communication. Communication is the element that not only gets the ball rolling for unlocking your productivity, but it is a must to help guide someone else! Dr. Steven Lifland, my finance professor: thank you for your lectures on "Timing". The opportunities in our lives come and go in an instant so we must not only be prepared for them but know how to use our resources to make the best of them! Dr. Bobby Hayes, my professor of English: thank you for pulling me aside that day after class and challenging me to give more of myself in my writing. You informed me that persistence will be the key in accomplishing your many educational endeavors. I have always trusted your red ink and critique on all of my major written assignments and I value all of your recommendations.

To my daughter Kennedy Alexis Goode: thank you for all of the incredible Post it notes you left on my desk to encourage me! When you came down those steps with that long pink Post it note with flowers on it, you gave me additional confidence to complete another page. I pray that you use this template to unleash more of your untapped potential one day and help others unleash theirs. Remember, Kennedy, your character is who you are when no one else is looking. Read chapter four on "Opportunities" over and over as you will have many of them. To my son Harrison Tate Mckinley Goode: please pay close attention to chapter four. Control 20 minutes a day and use it to think and dream! You have an incredible intuition, so use your visionary talents and abilities to their full potential. I know you will "Bet the Farm" when the time is right. Harrison, do not panic when you feel pressure! Just RRPD (Rehearse, Refine, Polish and Deliver), and I am certain you will do A-OK. Finally, to my incredible wife Andrea Lamone Goode: thank you for encouraging me to never doubt my leadership, enthusiasm and aggressive ambition. Your soft voice helps me every day to be a better husband, father and friend! The constant love that we share for our family's development is felt every day and we will press toward the mark with purpose in every step. You have been the glue to keep me on task and this book will be the start of the legacy that will help future generations of the Goodes; smooches!

In summary, the "thick skin" lessons, focus on quality, support for team development, professional presentation help, and innovation development has helped me become a better leader. My diverse client base over the past couple of decades has rewarded me with intangible experience! Thank you for believing that I would bring value to your respective organizations and allowing me to infuse energy, attitude, passion and power to your life as well. I will leverage all of these skills to help others unleash their full internal productivity and capture their dreams. Your contributions to my professional development will never be forgotten! We have what it takes to win; we can be more prepared today, so we can be confident to go for it all. Bet The Farm!

Thank you from the bottom of my heart,
Antwain

Introduction

"The 'key' to unlocking your unlimited potential is to let go of the past and summon your value-added support team to work on your future!"

- Antwain T. Goode

People are shaped by many internal and external factors. Having been raised by a single mother and a host of dynamic great aunts and uncles has given me a unique perspective on life. Growing up in the Fairfield Court public housing development in Richmond, Virginia was tough; however my mother was a hell of a lot tougher. The factor that dominates my perspective on life is the byproduct of my mother's determination, unyielding faith, and relentless passion: "tenacity!" I recall my mother telling me to outwork the competition, which is the foundation of my work ethic. Being the best at something requires a love for the process of fighting to develop *you*. My great aunts and uncles provided an incredible example of what teamwork looks like. Most only had third grade educations; however, they owned businesses, started churches in multiple states, and believed in rallying. I want to emphasize that your supporting cast can help you quickly forget past failures and setbacks and push you toward otherwise invisible opportunities. Bottom line: your supporting cast is your cheering section! Understanding productivity began early for me, as I "trained" under one of the greatest people professionals of all time: my aunt Veronica Morris. My aunt Veronica always taught the importance of maximizing your individual talents and abilities. Veronica would always say, "Use what you have because it is more than enough!" Life is all about people and getting those people to want to help you. Nothing in the world beats a good start—except for a shotgun start!

In order to start a fire you must be willing to cut some wood, strike a match and watch the spark become a blaze. The people in your life that gave you the value-added support are the logs. The logs have had the largest impact on you as they have shaped your values and principles. The match is your ambition. People go to sleep and dream. Dream big! Our ambitions can become reality if we add it to the logs. Put your logs to work for you. Your support system must be notified that you are serious about starting this fire, and you need their resources locked and loaded. Finally, the spark! Do something about it. I call "action" the all-important verb that sets the ball in motion. Combining the value-added logs, a match and a spark we can begin to get warm around the fire. We can recall who the best cooks are in the family and what dish they prepared that dazzled our taste buds. Unleashing productivity is no different! We have to use the best ingredients, the correct amount of flour (Love), the correct technique (Attitude), and the right flavoring (Character). Then, *viola*! –new opportunities, new visions; closed opportunities are now opened. New mentors will come to rally behind you all because of what you have put into the dish. Yum yum!

We are all in the same business: "sales." You can slice this pie any way you want to but I am convinced that we are all selling, buying or trading something when we interact with other people. Salespeople are not born sellers but are normal people who have an overabundance of curiosity, intuition, and optimism all wrapped in a high energy package. Get to business on the double quick. Success means, "Action!" It means relentless pursuit, unbreakable faith, openness to candor, good ol' horse sense, and spending quality time with your value-added team. You will then turn the key, open the door, and begin experiencing new personal gratification and robust life-altering opportunities.

You have what it takes today to make your tomorrow "Great!"

Theme: The Foundation

Successful leadership starts with "anchors."

> "You are a unique, unrepeatable miracle of God."
> -Kevin N. Earley, my best friend!

Leaders come and leaders go throughout our lives. The impact that individual relationships have on developing our identity strengthens or erodes our confidence. As such, leadership development is the first step in developing yourself and unlocking your uniqueness. How do you begin, where do you begin, and what are the steps one can take to spur leadership initiative? These are common questions about leadership development; and through education, experience, and training under some dynamic leaders, I have created a leadership model that can produce answers. Creating a leadership plan using leadership anchors will pave the way to evaluate values, ambition, time management, presentations, relationships, conflict resolution, and handling pressure. This chapter will leverage my model to examine six distinct knowledge areas of leadership: spirituality, passion, tenacity, vision, attitude, and power. The evaluation of these key knowledge areas provides the foundation for leadership initiative.

During the embryo stages of developing yourself and unlocking other areas of your mind you must be anchored. Hitting the ground running today cannot happen without increasing your confidence in your own uniqueness! Confidence begins before you start the job. The successful person begins winning by being thankful for what they have. The fact that you are unique and have extraordinary abilities must be visible to others: flowing out through your pores, in your gait, and sparkling in your eyes. Leaders are made, not born. I have been very fortunate to work under some extremely dynamic leaders, all of which are responsible for different parts of my development. You have some key champions that are responsible for what I call "The Big 6 Leadership Anchors". The anchors—Spirituality, Passion, Tenacity, Vision, Attitude, and Power—are tied to specific people in your life.

The people listed on the below chart are responsible for developing *my* core leadership abilities. You have or can build the same support system. I encourage you to use the following guide to write down your mentors in these areas. After you write them down call them, send them an email and/or write them a thank you note. These are the people who will boost your confidence and strengthen your core values! Remember that your sponsors will often come from various areas and levels of your life. Your first grade school teachers, high school coaches, grade school friends, pastors, relatives, college professors and executive client coaches are all acceptable! Choose the people to add to your Big 6 chart that are always in your corner and will always build you up. Your foundation for leadership greatness begins here. Building supercharged leadership does not come overnight; you must be anchored in order to lead. Begin strengthening your leadership now.

The Big 6 Leadership Key:

(1) Spirituality: The person in your life you most admire for peace/harmony.
(2) Passion: The person in your life you most admire for their determination.
(3) Tenacity: The person in your life with the most resilience: the "Never Quit," "Will Fight" spirit.
(4) Vision: The person in your life you most admire for their short or long range planning.
(5) Attitude: The person in your life you most admire for "Charged Emotion".

(6) Power: The person in your life you most admire for executing projects flawlessly and having "Mountain Moving" faith.

Antwain Goode's

<u>**Big 6 Core Leadership Anchors**</u>

Core Element	Name	Relationship	Called On The Phone	Sent Email	Thank You Note	Date Completed
(1) Spirituality	Kevin Earley	Best Friend	✓	✓	✓	11/7/2009
(2) Passion	Marva Goode	Mother	✓	✓	✓	11/7/2009
(3) Tenacity	Ed Smith	Fraternity Brother	✓	✓	✓	11/7/2009
(4) Vision	Tom Moore	Great Grand Father 95 yrs	In Heaven			1903-1998
(5) Attitude	Dora Shivers	Great Great Aunt 94 yrs	In Heaven			1915-2010
(6) Power	Robert Morris	Uncle U.S. Air Force	In Heaven			1948-2005

If your anchor has been called to heaven, they are still a valuable part of your foundation. You will find that you have a mentor closer than you think!

Unlock your Leadership power now! Take 30-40 minutes and call or email—and definitely send that "Thank You" note to—your support system! You are to spend a minimum of five minutes on each individual. The fact that you took the time to reach out to these people will add precious miles to your journey and will provide the mortar you will need to anchor your grand pillars of leadership. Keep it simple! If you do not have "thank you" notes, any loose-leaf sheets of paper will do!

It is the thought that counts, and count it will!

Here is your chart. Begin now!

The Big 6 Leadership Key:

(1) Spirituality: The person in your life you most admire for peace/harmony.

(2) Passion: The person in your life you most admire for their determination.

(3) Tenacity: The person in your life with the most resilience the "Never Quit," "Will Fight" spirit.

(4) Vision: The person in your life you most admire for their short range/long range planning.

(5) Attitude: The person in your life you most admire for "Charged Emotion".

(6) Power: The person in your life you most admire for executing projects flawlessly and having "Mountain Moving" faith.

(Insert your name here)

Big 6 Core Leadership Anchors

Core Element	Name	Relation ship	Called On The Phone	Sent Email	Thank You Note	Date Completed
(1)Spirituality						
(2)Passion						
(3)Tenacity						
(4)Vision						
(5)Attitude						
(6)Power						

Successful professional, your steps to leadership begin with thanking these incredible people!

Reach out to them and say, "Thank you!"

"Thank you" notes talk to the heart.

When was the last time you gave someone sincere appreciation? When was the last time you wrote that aunt or uncle who bought you a pop or took you to the movies? When was the last time you sent a thank you note to the receptionist who helped you set that appointment for a high profile client? When was the last time you wrote your pastor a note to say, "Keep up the good work"? Successful professional, all of these scenarios have one commonality, which is the failure to acknowledge the people who matter most. The success that you will receive in life will be equal to what you give in life. We have the opportunity to send a small token of appreciation at our fingertips and it will cost you a simple postage stamp: the great "thank you" note.

I started writing notes to family, friends and customers when I was 25. I was introduced to this form of appreciation when one of my managers (Dale Shoop) wrote me a note and left it on my desk one day after work. Dale was an incredible leader. This gentleman put me on my first plane trip for the company and gave me a pep talk so sincere that he could have given it to his own son. Dale always had a wonderful way to say "thank you", but the note that he left me was what made a lasting impression on my life. I walked into the office and saw this little note with my name on it. The note read: "You are doing a fine job, -Dale." Those six words meant so much to me because Dale Shoop was a very sincere and direct manager. A couple of weeks went by, as every night I saw Dale's note on my nightstand at home and felt inspired to send a note to someone in my family. I needed to tell them how much they meant to me. Emails and text messaging are convenient, but lack the warm heartfelt compassion of a handwritten note.

The handwritten note bespeaks honor, sincerity, and courage. Yes, courage! It takes courage to share your thoughts with another person. In order for you to be the best at your craft you must be willing at some point to tell the people who support you that you care. A good way to do that is to write them a special note. The people who receive your sincere good intentions will reward you with deep kindness in very surprising ways.

Here are some things to remember when writing a "thank you" note:

> ➢ Just Start! Write one (a blank sheet of paper, a napkin, or Post it note are all acceptable). Go!
> ➢ State a purpose (in detail, tell them why you are writing this sincere note and how they made you feel).
> ➢ Close your note properly (always close by re-stating your thoughtfulness).
> ➢ Be consistent (write at least one "thank you" note per month). You will touch the lives of twelve people a year.

Successful professional, remember that thoughtfulness is a large cog in the leadership machine.

Be kind to everyone you meet as everyone is going through some type of challenge.

Write a handwritten note today and it will blossom into a beautiful bouquet of roses in the near future!

You do not choose your mentors; your mentors choose you!

"Always be upfront and honest; never bullshit your way through life. Never try to serve someone cat shit and tell them that it is really butterscotch pudding."
-Ron Willard

I give a tremendous amount of credit to my past client mentors. What all of these managers and myself share is the ability to recognize uniqueness. The client mentor who further developed my intuition to recognize quality was Ron Willard. One of my showroom employees walked into my office and informed me that a very unique client needed technical support. I walked through the warehouse showroom and Chris yelled "Mr. Goode, we're over here." I walked over and introduced myself to Ron Willard of RJ Reynolds Tobacco Company. Ron had a presence that reminded me of a couple of important people in my life: my uncle Robert Morris and my uncle Donald Moore, both of whom served in the U.S. Air Force. Both of these men had incredible stage presence and commanded attention in any room because of their remarkable characters. The Sicilian looking gentleman with curly hair gave a very polite greeting to me. "Well how are you Mr. Goode? I am Mr. Ron Willard of RJ Reynolds Tobacco." The immediate show of professional respect to my employee, myself and my organization was clearly felt. I asked Ron what could we do to assist him and he said "I am looking for a special flashlight."

Now! Who would think that a request as simple as looking for a flashlight would be the request that changed the branding, perception and capabilities of my branch in Winston-Salem, NC? Successful professional, never think of small opportunities as small opportunities—think of them as needle-in-a-haystack chances of hitting the million dollar lotto.

The solution for Mr. Willard was not found that day. The flashlight that he wanted was not to be found. I enthusiastically gave it my best and the client was pleased with the tag team customer service. Ron's comment was: "You guys made a great presentation for your company as I swore I would never come in here again based on the last experience that I had." My reply: "Ron, there is a new cowboy in town and his name is Antwain Goode!" Ron smiled and replied, "I am sure we will meet again." Within a couple of months of my chance meeting with Ron I was promoted to Account Management and guess whose account was in my package? RJ Reynolds Tobacco! What is so ironic about this chance encounter is that I only had one business card for this incredibly large client; it was that of Ron Willard.

Unleashing your energy, attitude, passion and power has a direct effect on others as they too want to work with productive, polished people. I will never forget visiting Ron Willard at the Whittaker Park Manufacturing Facility with no appointment and no phone call. I just showed up with one single thought on my mind: "I will give it my all in trying to help someone solve a problem and make their job easier." The front desk receptionist Mrs. Mary Watts was on duty. Remember that everyone has a stake in your development! You have a chance for opportunity to knock with every encounter. Mrs. Watts made the comment, "Young man, you look very handsome with your tie and jacket." I warmly thanked her for the pleasant comment and asked where I could find Mr. Willard. Mrs. Watts commented "Ron is just first class and lives by the golden rule." Awesome people are known by what other people say about them and not what they say about themselves.

Ron walked up to me in the lobby in amazement. He asked what I was doing there. I said, "I got a promotion and you are my client. You no longer have to come to my organization for solutions, your solutions specialist can come to you!" Ron's comment: "You are in the right place at the right time." What happened after that point was simply amazing. The relationship between Ron and I grew and so did the visibility of my organization. The incredible people at RJ Reynolds Tobacco groomed me in some very incredible ways. Learning how to service a powerhouse manufacturing client like RJ Reynolds takes a great deal of character, confidence and persistence. Without a doubt they are responsible for thickening my skin. Ron was one of the best supply chain leaders I have ever met. Ron not only helped develop me but pushed me to be bold in meeting other high powered RJ Reynolds leaders. It was that push that made me set an appointment with a second mentor, who I humbly admire for setting an example of what I could one day aspire to be.

The gentle giant who has truly blessed my life was Mr. Tommy Hickman, Sr. Vice President of Operations of RJR Tobacco. Successful professional, hear me well: "You do not choose your mentors; your mentors choose you!" Setting an appointment with a Sr. Vice President is a serious endeavor to say the least. You have to have confidence if you want to win in this thing called life. When I received the email from Tommy I said "Oh wow! He is going to meet with me." I immediately started to get all of my ducks in a row, and performed all of the necessary diagnostics that I could on how I would be able to serve his organization. What happened that day at the RJR Tobaccoville plant in King, NC was life changing. When I met Tommy's secretary, Mrs. Linda Jones, she looked at me and said "Young man who are you here to see?" My reply: "Mr. Hickman!" Mrs. Jones did not call him on his phone but instead walked into his office and said "There is a young professional here to see you." I had never met Tommy before but Ron had informed me just how polished he was, and warned me to have my stuff together.

Ron did not pull any punches when his reputation was on the line. When I walked into his office I had to fight to keep my composure as I had never walked into an office that big before. The office was like a corner lot in a subdivision. I can remember those big windows wrapped all around the yellow loveseat, and the seating area I found extremely inviting. I did not know if I was in an office or in a country club sitting room. My guard was completely down and Tommy said: "Mr. Goode, please come and sit over here." Tommy was sitting behind this big desk, smoking a big cigar and signing a stack of employee thank you cards. I thought to myself, "Wow: first class stuff." How humble, a man on this level who has a heart for his subordinates. Tommy gave me a quote that day which I will never forget. The quote was to always "Go in as a lamb and leave as a lion!" Successful professional, you must continue to dream big. Sitting in that big office and being mentored by so polished a professional was something that I have envisioned in my dreams. The Lord arranged my life to meet him and to get a first glimpse of what I may become. Your dreams can be realities and the people that you meet are not coincidental. Meeting Mr. Hickman added a unique dynamic to my life as he not only endorsed me but charismatically let me know there is more opportunity out there than I could ever imagine. The mentorship lessons led to community board membership opportunities and opened previously invisible doors to personal philanthropic development.

Where would successful professionals be without client coaches? Successful professional, you must always have your antenna up for mentors. You must be intuitive and inquisitive! Do not be afraid to turn over that mentor rock as there may be buried treasure laying there. That is just what happened to me that day, when I turned over that rock. I found gold in the form of mentor "character" development.

Here are my top tips for building client trust and sustained mutual respect:

- ➤ Be on time! (Ron Willard taught me this the hard way!) Do not leave the door open for your competition!
- ➤ People want to work with people who have guts! (Grab the bull by the horns).
- ➤ People want "make it happen" people around them. (Tenacity is needed to get the ball rolling).
- ➤ Know some folks! (Clients want to work with people with resources).
- ➤ Get turned on! (The key to networking is the referral). Networking builds your reputation!

Successful professional, go above and beyond in servicing others and your reputation will go above and beyond as well.

You do not choose your mentors! Your mentors choose you!

Plant your feet; get an advanced degree!

"Leadership and confidence should always sit in the front seat
with you as you drive along life's highway!"
-Dr. Alberta Haynes Herron

Successful professionals experience majestic Eiffel Tower highs and Dead Sea lows. Many sales professionals have not been coached in how to handle unavoidable lows. You never forget the feeling of being on the tip top of your profession. Colleagues from all around the country and the world see your success. The plaques are engraved with your name on them and your certificates of achievement will be stacked high. However, just when things are going incredibly awesome, you will feel a certain tremor in the floor. You guessed it! A seismic life earthquake will be coming your way.

Client closings, lost contracts, physical challenges, family emergencies, emotional stress and lost champions can destroy your morale. You are first class and are rich in life "quality." The organization that once handed you all of those plaques and accolades may one day ask "What have you done for me lately?" Successful professional, I tell you the truth, it is lonely at the top and lonely at the bottom. Where can one go to recover, re-examine, and build better strategies not only at work but in life? Who can help you get over these small hurdles that seem like 100-foot tsunami tidal waves? I know of a grand solution. "Get your advanced degree now!" I am a business major so my answer was an MBA (Master of Business Administration). Successful professional, whatever your undergraduate degree was in, go back NOW for additional training! Let the classes begin.

One of the most critical decisions I have ever made in my life and for my family was to pursue an advanced degree. Burnout can creep up in the weirdest ways. Burnout can impair your visibility of your big dreams and aspirations. You must always have your personal goals in sight. You spend eight to ten hours every day working; you must give equal diligence to your personal dreams or they will never come to fruition. I took a floater one Monday morning focused with relentless determination to start a program. The university that was destined for me was about to close their admissions process. I wanted to prove I was one of the best professionals in my organization, that I was a sharp business professional and that I really knew business. Successful professional, there are people in the world that you have to meet and people in the world who need to meet you. Well, that Monday I met someone alright: Dr. Alberta Haynes Herron, Founding Dean of the Norcross Graduate School.

Successful professional, you need professors! I had no idea what I was to expect out of the program. I knew I was bringing a tremendous amount of leadership, managerial experience, and exposure from working with many high profile industrial clients to the program. What I did not know were the incredible critical thinkers that were waiting for me when I got there. The Norcross Graduate School at High Point University employs incredibly talented professors who re-engineered my problem solving capabilities. Successful professional, keep in mind that whatever the number of classes you have to take to complete the program, so will be the number of possible professor mentors you will have! Mentors are God's gift to people who are passionate about love, service, and commitment. A mentor of mine, Mr. Alvin Jefferson gave me some sincere instruction about mentorship. Alvin's comment: "What one needs in life to win are a Mentor, a Tutor and a Sponsor." Alvin concluded, "It is rare to ever have all three in one person." Alvin was right! It is rare to have all three in one. The Lord has really blessed me as I found such a person who fulfilled all three requirements, and her name is Dr. Alberta Haynes Herron.

Ms. Linda Mae Hill, the administrative assistant, was sitting behind the desk that Monday and saw fire in my eyes. Ms. Mae Hill, who I now call "Aunt Mae," summoned Dr. Herron from her desk to meet me. Again, I was totally thrown off guard, as I am about 5'8" with my cowboy boots on, and out came Dr. Herron, a 6 foot 1 elegant, polished educator with eyes of an eagle. My question to Dr. Herron on the spot was this: "What do I need to do to get into this program?" Successful professional, you must draw a line in the sand sometimes in your life. Dr. Herron then stretched out her wings and informed me of the rigorous program of Norcross, accompanied by the comment "What you get out of anything is what you put into it!"

Successful professional, your professor mentors do not owe you anything. So, in order to have a friend and possible mentor you must first show yourself as friendly. My tutoring began when Dr. Herron began sharing powerful words of wisdom which gave me extra oomph! I can recall a great life lesson when we talked about the importance of controlling 20 minutes a day and to use those 20 minutes to "Think and to Dream!" Our conversations were intense as she made it perfectly clear that we all have opportunities each day but there are those who just do not want to take advantage of them. Successful professional, you must hold yourself to high standards if you want others to deliver high standards to you. Indeed, you too must look for these attributes in your mentors. You have an incredible opportunity and responsibility as a mentee. Always be on time for your appointments together, research relevant topics to keep your mentors fresh, and look the part! You are a direct representation of them.

2

Theme: Values

What is your "Mission Statement?"

Have you ever noticed the confidence level of high performing people? We look at these people in awe because of their special talents and abilities. The thoughts that run through our minds are: "How did they do it?", "What resources did they have?", "There is no way that can be done", and "Just amazing!" We can achieve the same success if we have a rock solid personal mission statement. Your mission statement is your personal constitution. Just as each word of the Declaration of Independence anchors our nation, so will your mission statement anchor you! The mission statement that you will create must be worn as a badge of truth, courage and integrity. Your success in unlocking productivity will be a reflection of your personal mission statement. People from all around the world will see your badge as a lighthouse and run to safety. Take a look at my mission statement and we will workshop how to create one for you.

<u>My Personal Mission Statement</u>

- *I am nothing, but Christ in me makes me something.*
- *I will fight ferociously for my family and stay committed.*
- *I will show them persistence, compassion and consideration at all times.*

- *I shall not fear any man on earth!*
- *I shall fear only God.*
- *I shall make sure that my influence on others is consistent with my values and principles so that my legacy will breed a legacy.*
- *Therefore, I so choose as my mission to stand on my "Rock" and wait.*

Antwain T. Goode
Lafayette, Louisiana
June 30, 1998 10:35 am

Now you may be asking yourself where on earth to begin. Your mission statement has already been written for you, so let's unlock it now and write it down. The leadership core elements will help you get started.

Write a sentence using each of the leadership core elements:

[(1) Spirituality, (2) Passion, (3) Tenacity, (4) Vision, (5) Attitude, and (6) Power]

1. I am in harmony when I do what? *Pray, read, meditate, think, and love.*
2. I am passionate about what? *Serving others and giving.*
3. What fuels my determination? *Family, failure, love, spiritual wealth, material wealth, support.*
4. What do you believe in? Where do you want to go? *Believe you can get to your destination.*
5. I am motivated the most by what? What energizes you? *Inspiration.*
6. What is it in you that nothing can stop? What is your victory and execution statement? *I will get it done!*

I want you to know that your mission statement can be one word, one sentence or a combination of both. Nike used only three words to determine its brand: "Just Do It!"

Stop and take 30 minutes to write down the words that will anchor your life! Let's create your leadership badge of courage now. You, your family, future generations and people around the world will reap the rewards from your personal mission statement. Write a sentence for each element and *voila*! You will have your mission statement. GO!!!

1. Spirituality_____
2. Passion_____
3. Tenacity_____
4. Vision_____
5. Attitude_____
6. Power_____

After completion, frame your mission statement on your wall and memorize!

Congratulations!!!

You must have "Passion."

Passion is a powerful force in making our dreams a reality. My mother is an incredible woman. I remember being the Master of Ceremony at her 60th birthday celebration. I made a statement that defines passion as it relates to her unwavering faith raising my three siblings and I: "A mother's love will cause her to walk 1,000 miles for her child." I am always grateful for seeing that spark in my mother's eyes as it has truly been a guiding force to fuel my passion and I am forever thankful to her for it! My mother showed me that with passion any wall can be cracked, knocked down, climbed over, blown up or detoured around.

Successful professional, unlocking and harnessing this powerful emotion will differentiate you. Passion will cause you to explore uncharted areas of the mind and discover new opportunities on deserted islands. Please keep in mind that passion is an amplified emotion and can be taken as overconfidence or flat out pushiness. Managing passion is like driving a five speed. You have to press down on the clutch and accelerator with balanced force. Taking your feet off of one or the other too fast will cause you to move too fast or the car will just cut off!

Successful professional, you have passion and it is a must if you want to reach your full potential. You want to convincingly stand out. I can tell you that there are many competitive vultures out there that are out to capture your business. Remember as your passion grows so will your tolerance for lackluster performance. You will not STAND FOR IT! You strive to be the best and you deserve the best. My career has shown me that it is easy to take your eye off the ball. One very big misconception for professionals is that they often think that they are the only ones who have passion. Our clients are also very passionate! Your job is to use your passion to ignite their passion! If you complete your task here you will move closer to that magical pot of gold that I call "Client Loyalty".

Here are some examples of how to drive your five speed passion Lamborghini!

"The Clutch"	"The Gas"	Your Lamborghini can Move!!
Successful Professional's Passion List	The Client's Passion List	Comments from the client will be:
Be passionate about your suite of value added services. These services will help your client overachieve on their goals.	The client needs your help to bring their ideas to life. The customer will win and you will win loyalty.	CEO/Presidents = "We are happy to have a professional who remains loyal to our needs."
Be passionate about delivering your obligations to your organization. Bottom line: "Be responsible". The more responsible you are, the more the client will be responsible for helping you hit your targets!!!	The client needs your help to identify solutions to their financial objectives and quarterly strategies.	CEO/Presidents = "WOW! Our professional cares about us. We saved $$ on multiple strategic projects! Let's give our specialist a larger project."
Be passionate about creating wealth for your family! Spiritual wealth, knowledge-based wealth, leadership-based wealth, and a few extra coins in the piggy bank will suit you just fine!	The client wants to grow in every area, department, and initiative that they can. They need you and your core elements to assist multiple areas of their business. Become a cog in as many machines that you can!	CEO/Presidents ="Let's reward our professional because of their passion and service" $$$$$$$$$$$

Passion will always force you out of your comfort zone. The more determined you are to achieve your goals the more passion octane will kick in to get you there.

Your Lamborghini is ready! Adding Passion + proper clutch/gas harmony, you will deliver high productivity performance.

Zoom, Zoom, Zoom!!!

Become your hero today.

"No one knows what you are working on, on the inside."
- Glenn Mabe, Winston-Salem, YMCA

Successful professional, you have taken the steps to re-invent yourself so now let's discuss how you can become your own hero. Our lives are shaped by people. We all know or have seen people that simply defy the odds of losing. Our heroes come from many backgrounds and various disciplines. The people that we admire have abilities that promote the betterment of humanity and leave a lasting mark on mankind. Successful professional, the people that we call heroes are just like you! You too have hero powers and we will unlock those today.

The following section on heroes is designed to help you dial into the values, principles and work ethics of our bona fide leaders. Again, these people put their shoes on the same as you do; they have faced their own sets of circumstances and have had to fight for their incredible achievements. Sometimes we need to look into the lives of others in order to unlock the strength within ourselves. All you need is one or two people believing in you, and you believing in yourself. Your confidence should be rock solid as you know God's arms are always wrapped around you.

Becoming your hero first begins with being totally honest with yourself about the motives of your hero. What is your hero all about? You should have a clear understanding of the motivators of your hero and their short and long term strategies. Do the homework to find out their family history and details of their childhood and past. You want to search for the "Aha" moments in their lives that are similar to yours. The area in their life that is the most similar to yours will be the starting point for you.

You might think to yourself "I will never meet my hero" as they may be deceased, in another country, a high ranking political figure, actor and so on. So what do you do to meet your hero? You start by researching people that are in your city, town, family and community arenas that have similar accolades. Bottom line: if you cannot physically touch your hero, choose an alternative nearby and meet them! You will be surprised at the many new relationships you will make by reaching out to heroic figures in your own community. The path that you travel will give you confidence. The people that you meet will see your ambitions and will ride with you on your quest to help you fulfill your dreams. The hero that is in you is just waiting to be unleashed. Once you have developed your own heroic abilities, you can then use your power to infuse hope, determination, and confident risk taking into others. Yes, confident risk taking! Heroes are bold, courageous and ambitious. Do not be afraid to go for the gusto. You have one life to live so live it with courage and conviction. In order to win in today's marketplace you will need dramatic confidence and vast vision. Become the hero you have always wanted to be today.

Come on "Hero"–show up now, and save the day!

Character!

"Good character is more praised than outstanding talent."
-Vincent Medel, my friend

Bet the Farm was written to unlock the unlimited productivity inside of people. Our character shapes how we are viewed by others as well as our ability to capture opportunities. People are checking you out constantly. You can ill afford to take chances on your personal brand. Unlocking the untapped potential within you is about maximizing your talents and abilities. You will have a sustained competitive advantage if you continue to use all of the weapons that are at your disposal. Your mission statement will be the quintessential element in unlocking all of your amazing potential. Use your mission statement to shield you from negativity and to build confidence in future endeavors. The last ingredient that is needed to unlock your new success is character.

Who you are and what you will become are all determined when no one else is looking. Planting flowers with your children, a family picnic, mentoring a college student, and visiting a nursing home are all character builders. Character is what separates the good, better and best in people. People with character listen well, laugh often and love much. At the end of the day you want to feel proud and confident that you gave it your best and other people benefited from it. Remember it is better to give than to receive and creativity is better than knowledge. Follow the tools that I have mentioned in this book and make the most out of the time you have on earth every day.

Remember: no regrets! Your dreams are at your grasp. Grab them!

3

Theme: Ambition

Attitude: "The breakfast of champions"!

> "*Commitment*—it's the difference between those who attain success and those who dream of it!"
> -Antwain T. Goode

The all-powerful "attitude"! We notice people every day who display a certain zeal for life. These people live each day as if it were their last. Guess what? We are compelled to support these individuals because of their energetic, attractive nature. What type of fuel will you use to fire up your spirit and move your body like a runaway freight train? Successful professional, let me roll out the red carpet on this topic as "attitude" deserves a grand entrance. A person's attitude is the caffeine for motivating others. Building a strong attitude is just like growing a flower.

My formula for growing this flower is as follows:

The Pot=Love (Treat everyone with respect!) It will warm your spirit and warm theirs.
The Soil=Giving (Give more of you!) Your clients will give you more opportunities.
The Stem=Humility (Be Thankful!) You cannot get there by yourself.

The Petals=Hunger (Fight for your family!) You do want to eat, don't you?
The Seed=Mission (Strive for execution!) Do it right every time.
The Sun Rays=Desire (Develop a relentless pursuit to solve customer challenges.) Keep Trying!

Building attitude muscle will give you the strength to tackle complex challenges. People will be motivated to work with you because of the vast blooms on your flower. People that have glowing attitudes are given a shot right off the bat. A person's appearance, smile, walk, and smell—yes, smell—play a huge part in how a person is perceived. Perceptions are real and we must take them seriously. Your attitude should infiltrate the room and remain in the room when you exit. People who have great attitudes tend to deposit their attractive nature into others. Make a deposit! Yes, we are to make investments into the lives of others. Your attitude has your character imbedded in it as well.

When people say you have a great attitude they are also complimenting everything about you! Carry your warm, compassionate and persistent attitude with you at all times. Remember that with love you have a great home; with giving you make future rewards, with humility you never boast, with a clear mission you will not miss your target, with hunger you will always be persistent and with the rays of desire you will fight for new ground!

Plant your flower today!

The Determined.

"It is a sad day to be remembered by what you could have been or should have been, but didn't!"
-Ted Leggett, Winston-Salem, YMCA

The determined always show great resolve! Have you ever noticed how a determined person walks? The steps that are taken are deliberate, forward and with even strides. Rain or shine, the "determined" will reap the rewards of 80% of the market share by owning the preferred position with 20% of their clients. Determination, not luck, is what closes large opportunities. The skeptics and naysayers will always make comments like "Robin was lucky to land that client" or "Dan had that project just land in his lap." No! Do not believe that for a second. Winning in any organization starts with a positive mindset! The strongest weapon a person has is the complex machine called the "mind."

Success in life comes from one's ability to psychologically visualize the desired state. Successful professional, you have the keys to unlock any door if you believe you have the master key. Clients want people on the team who have determination and passion. The combined forces generate incredible momentum. Clients today have multiple strategic teams and need successful professionals that can communicate and remove ineffective processes.

Determination is a great internal weapon for attaining any goal. I recall many corporate procurement manager meetings that built confidence in my character and shaped my brand. I recall a mile long stretch of no's on cost savings ideas, supplier reduction initiatives, and value added solutions. The directors of procurement had the keys to the BMW and I was determined to take a drive. Successful professionals, no matter what the obstacle you have in your respective lives remember to "never stop trying!" Never stop believing in yourself and your unique talents. Keep in mind that you are not always the customer and you must be willing to serve. You have to be as equally determined to give as you are to get! There is a concomitant bond between the two; you cannot have one without the other. Fight for your opportunities with zest and zeal and do not squander time in the process.

Time is the element that you cannot get back as you move to attain your goals. Successful professional, give your time and talents to the people who want them. You will not be able to inject your leadership into everyone so do not try to. You have strong spiritual awareness and a quality mission statement that will cause your life to overflow with people trying to help you attain your goals. Determination must be infused into your daily diet of success. Victory begins when determination spikes are plated into the side of a mountain (the goal). Keep your eyes fixed on the top of the mountain. Never, ever quit!

Here are my top determination tips:

> **Dream big:** Replay your victorious dream over and over in your mind until it becomes reality.
> **Get up early:** Do not squander time! Have a purposeful plan for your day. Ask a member of your value added support team to be your morning prayer partner.
> **Build a good team:** You need to get the right people on the bus, the wrong people off the bus, and a good bus driver before you can let the bus roll.
> **Never quit:** Be resilient and show great resolve when you are up against trouble. Meet it face-to-face and wear down that trouble.

➢ **Smell the roses:** Life is short, so take the time to enjoy your hard work. Many would love to have one more day, a few more hours or a couple more minutes of life!

➢ **Motivate someone else:** You have an obligation to help someone else become more determined to pursue their goals. Give support and it will be given back unto you!

Determination will take you and your family to higher heights. Successful professional, set the road ablaze with passion. The Lord will dispatch angels to protect your every step!

I run straight to the goal with purpose in every step.
1 Corinthians 9:26

Creativity!

We can create what we do not have by focusing on the unseen vs. the seen. Faith comes to mind when I think of creativity. To be as productive as one need be in this new fast paced global economy will require "off the roof top ideas." Successful professional, you can ill afford to allow anyone to throw cold water on your dreams and visionary ideas. Creativity will be necessary as you encounter unique speed bumps, road blocks, and brick walls. When do we most use creativity? We use creativity when we are short on resources. The less we have of something, the more we need to gather up the materials from somewhere. Successful professional, you should take the offensive as often as possible when using creativity. Anticipate change and start brainstorming! Now, let's work on how to unlock your creative juices.

Creativity spawns from the things we like to do. We all have different talents and abilities and those abilities will help you with your ideas and "Aha" moments. In order to capitalize on your creative ideas you must not be afraid to stumble a few times. See the stumble as the trigger for determination (more on this in chapter 10). Your ideas and dreams have been brewing in your mind and spirit for a long time, but were never acted upon. You must boldly proclaim that your ideas are not only good but great! If you do not think your idea is great and worthy of action, no one will. What if the Wright brothers had stopped dreaming that they could fly? Hmm…I think you get my drift.

Successful professional, leadership involves a great deal of creativity. The sooner you free yourself of the routine mindset the sooner you will be developing revolutionary ideas. The cross functional teams that you will build will look to you to set the standard for business development. Empower your teams to have monthly game/creativity sessions. The possibilities are limited only by your imagination—you could use a master Lego building set, team brain twisters, etc. You could even build a house together through Habitat for Humanity. You as a leader must always strive for a sense of unity as you create new antidotes. Have some fun! Listen to your teams, laugh with your teams, and share unconditional love for them. You must show confidence in other peoples' ability to come up with great ideas.

Here are my top tips for unleashing creativity:

> **Re-Invent your cooking!**
> (Subscribe to a cooking magazine. Change your diet and try new meals.)
> **Visit a museum or see a theatrical performance.**
> (Once a quarter visit your local museum or see a new performance to gain new perspectives.)
> **Mentor someone.**
> (Mentor a college student and share experiences—trust me, me you will learn so much from a mentee and vice versa.)
> **Get a journal.**
> (Write down your thoughts as they contain your dreams.)
> **Listen to music.**
> (Set aside 30 minutes a week and listen to new sounds. Try country, jazz, opera, reggae, Latino, rock, classical, gospel or easy listening.) Expand your mind to new forms of musical art.

➤ **Visit your library.**
(Once a month visit your main library and check out documentaries on your heroes.) Libraries are free! Save some money and check out books, movies and new tunes!

Successful professional, you are incredibly creative!

Do not let anyone, not even yourself, talk you out of your "aha" moments. Try something new today!

4

Theme: Time Management

9 **to 5 is not enough; 6 to 6 is a must.**

Hickory, dickory, dock, you must work around the clock! There are two types of people in the world; people that let things happen and people that make things happen. The *9 to 5* Dolly Parton song was a great tune, but if you try to play that song out in real life your competition will clean your clock! Status quo is not an option for you. Productivity is increased by proper use of time! Getting up earlier and staying up later is possible with well-orchestrated personal planning. I know what separates excellent, good and average: the answer is commitment. The more time you invest, the more opportunities you will have to build your personal brand!

Let's talk about 6:00 am to 6:00 pm. Working in the field of Industrial Distribution has been very rewarding. My industrial clients are the salt of the earth. I have been fortunate to serve this sector for over 25 years in various capacities. My clients all have varied shifts: 1st, 2nd and 3rd. I would argue that there is one shift that I have grown to love a little more than the others, and it is 3rd. The men and women who work this shift know perseverance and value leadership. I remember working on a project for a large manufacturer and I had to meet the 3rd shift management team. Jeff Watts, Larry Mccan and George Pilcher were great clients, mentors and friends to me.

Let's first discuss Jeff Watts! Jeff informed me that the best Account Managers can meet their customers on the "damn moon" if they have an opportunity. Jeff Watts always made time for me because I was passionate about delivering new industry changing solutions that would make productivity easier for his teams. Clients like Jeff want individuals who will not be afraid to push the envelope and if need be set the envelope on fire! One of Jeff's favorite comments was "Are you a damn chicken or do you wear kerosene rags around your ankles to keep the fire ants off your ass?" The moral of that question is just "Make decisive and bold decisions." Jeff is a straight up client and that's the type of feedback that you want. As I look back, I know what made it easy to call on that 3rd shift. Well, I love getting up in the morning (5:30 am). In my backyard in Winston-Salem, NC I have a bird house hanging on my dogwood tree and at 5:30 each morning the birds chirp along and wake me up. I informed Jeff, "I'm a cowboy—we rise earlier than the sun."

I remember getting fired up to meet Larry Mccan at King Barbeque at 4:30 am for dinner; I am talking about a fun, early, early morning business dinner. Larry would coach me up on hand tools and what effect they had on productivity and the bottom line. Larry pushed the envelope of my inner drive and gave great tutelage on how to view, service, and retain large clients. Larry made the point that global organizations run around the clock and your breakfast, lunch and dinner times will vary. So I had to move with the cheese and remember that it is cocktail hour somewhere around the world. You have to be bold to meet the needs of your clients! The relationship that Larry and I formed at 4:30 am was an incredible character builder. Larry had expectations on service no matter what the time. So I was on time, every time.

My clients re-engineered how I thought about time and enhanced my work discipline. Re-engineering your work patterns to meet your clients will pay large dividends as your clients will notice your tenacity and work ethic! George Pilcher was the last musketeer of the graveyard shift. George was the client who mentored me with the fewest words but also with the most elegant words. What I learned from George was to never stop being persistent! That's right! Keep trying and keep fighting. George has a very pleasant and calming demeanor. George, at 4:30 am, said to me: "Antwain, you are one step closer to an opportunity because you got out of your bed early to make an opportunity." What a clear statement! You have to get up early and make it happen. George is one incredible client mentor. His words are few but the content is irreplaceable.

Working in management for over 10 years has given me the privilege to be mentored by some awesome people and of course there are some that set you up for greatness. Great leadership is seen and not just heard. No one could beat him to work, no one knew the numbers better than he did, and no one knew his clients like he did. JD Knight had all of these awesome leadership attributes and most importantly he loved his people and their families. What I learned was fantastic "brick and mortar" leadership. JD to me, was like a John Wooden of Industrial Distribution.

I remember JD keeping an early morning/late evening schedule and it provided a very good template to further develop my work ethic. Individual development was always in the forefront of his mind as he worked to enhance our unique talents. JD gave more respect than anyone could give him. I will never forget the day I was promoted to manager at the age of 25 and I was working under JD for manager training. JD was excited for me and also gave me the ultimate one-two punch rules. He said, "Antwain, rule number one: never let anyone out work you" and "rule number two: get up early and stay late!" JD was the best and that wisdom has helped me in every endeavor. So you heard the man. Do not be out worked and do not let anyone out work you! Amen to that. Do you think that Donald Trump shuts it down at 5:00 or the best basketball player in the world stops shooting free throws when practice is over? Chances are slim to none. Anyone who wants to be great will spend the appropriate time in the appropriate places.

Time management is critical and attention to the clock will help you meet deadlines, fulfill promises, and avoid time snares. Controlling productivity requires successful time management strategies at home as well as at work. Indeed, organizations have constructs that corral your time to meet shareholder expectations, but you can also create stronger mutual work life balance by developing heightened time sensitivity awareness at home. Personal wellbeing is very important and controlling your time at home will give you more time to target new dreams and ideas. Carefully crafting time management goals for you and your family will help you properly evaluate where time should be added or removed for select tasks.

Organize your plans for tomorrow today!

The following tips can help you control the clock before and after work:

Early Morning Jump Start (Critical Time in Building Productivity)

➢ Enjoy early morning prayer/meditation time. Give thanks!
➢ Eat some breakfast.
➢ Have a go to work chant! (The Lord will help us win! We are the Goodes.)
➢ Children's go to school chant! (What's gonna work? Teamwork!)
➢ Always kiss and hug your significant other and family before you go to work.

Evening Family Time (Critical Time for Listening and Planning)

➢ Listen to your children and what they have learned today.
➢ Enjoy your dinner as a family (no TV).
➢ Exercise.
➢ Reinforce "teamwork" with your children. Create a come home from school to do list!
➢ Everyone get their clothes out for tomorrow.
➢ Tell your significant other you love them (and listen).
➢ Purchase a calendar for your children and allow them to talk about their time management challenges. Let's help them manage their time more creatively!
➢ Create a mid-week plan to organize family chores and take back the weekend.

Late Evening (Critical Time for Reflection)

➢ Have the coffee pot or kettle locked and loaded for the morning.
➢ Invest in some comfortable PJ's. (Go to sleep in style!)
➢ Go to sleep and dream big!!!!!!

Work Week Time Management Ideas
(Remove Unexpected Work Time Traps)

➢ Take your lunch to work!
➢ Create a clear agenda for all appointments, meetings, and individual encounters.
➢ When managing complex projects, evaluate your relationships with others. Share mutual responsibility for deadlines to avoid re-work and stimulate partnership/comradeship.
➢ De-clutter your notes daily and write one "Thank you" note to someone!

All of these steps can be somewhat intertwined but not omitted. Success in unlocking your productivity begins with being conscious of time.

Oh yeah! Invest in a $5 digital cooking timer. Use the timer when ever you need to be on pin point accuracy. Boldly go in time management where you have never gone before.

Control your time. 6:00 am to 6:00 pm is a must!

Control 20 minutes a day. Use it to THINK and DREAM!

"In order to get what you have never had you have to do
what you have never done!"
-Damien Penn, Winston Salem, YMCA

The distinguishing factor between good and great could be how one spends a simple 20 minutes. We all have an incredible machine that has incredible power: it is called the mind. Your subconscious speaks to you all the time. I am convinced that day by day, our thoughts, words and actions create stepping stones to our successes. Our thoughts have a significant impact on helping us reach our desired state. So we need to maximize the time to "think and to dream!" Successful professional, let me tell you what could happen if you do not stop and take control of at least 20 minutes a day. Your life could be run by someone who does not care about your dreams or aspirations. By not taking control, you will look back over your life with regrets! Controlling 20 minutes a day will give you an advantage.

You may first realize that you've never implemented a strategy for all of the incredible visions you had lying in bed at night. You wake up in the morning invigorated and ready to begin your invention, write your book, lose the weight, get married, get your degree, or be a millionaire. You are on target and ready to begin when distraction creeps its way into your morning. Distractions are normal but you have to be focused on controlling just 20 minutes. Your dreams will become realities only if you keep them in front of you and touch them daily until you gain momentum. We all have friends and people in our families that have worked jobs for thirty or forty years for some company or institution who now spend the remaining balance of their lives attempting to re-create the lost time. Successful professional, you can have your cake and eat it too if you work just as hard for yourself as you do for your organization!

You may be asking yourself "Where am I going to find 20 minutes a day?" My answer will be that you can't *find* 20 minutes a day. "You *take* 20 minutes a day!" Successful professional, if you do not start taking your time to "think and to dream" you will be helping someone else stifle your hopes and dreams. I have elaborated on the dreams and now will address the thinking! We have so many obstacles that impede our path to success, but if we take some time to think we can lay out a good roadmap for success. We are incredible! We have brains! We are critical thinkers! There are people out there who want to make you feel that you are not capable. Let me make it clear to you; you are more than capable and have incredible gifts and abilities. The time that you spend working for companies and institutions implementing their strategies and campaigns should be blended with your own ambitions, goals and dreams. Successful professional, you can strengthen your critical thinking by creating a daily journal for yourself and one for your profession. Time waits for no one! The longer you prolong implementation of your visions and dreams the less time you will have on the back end of your life to fulfill them.

> "A man is only as great as his mind."
> -Octavio Yepez, My good friend from Cuba

Use the following tips to control 20 minutes a day as it will add 20 years to your life!

- ➢ Get up 20 minutes early every morning (use it for solitude or prayer).
- ➢ Write down your visionary dreams. (Do not talk yourself out of your dreams! Make it happen.)
- ➢ Take a nap (yes, find the time and power rest and recapture your dreams daily).
- ➢ Take the time to "think." (You have a strong mind! Create a personal and professional to do list.)
- ➢ Find a place of solitude (find sanctuaries in different parts of your city). Pray and dream!

Successful professional, do not live your life with regrets; those thoughts of what you could have been, should have been or would have been but didn't.

Take the 20 minutes and it will give you 20 more years!!

Take good notes! Be a good secretary.

Historical data can be a great indicator of the future, but without good notes you will not have the necessary data to make sound predictions. Top professionals ply their trade with excellent note taking. Note taking is a lost art for some. Successful professional, you must be organized and able to decode client information and translate it to a desired solution. You will meet multiple clients on a daily basis, so create a database of all contact names and nicknames. "Know it all." Why should a potential client have to tell you their name twice? If you are a successful professional, they will not forget yours! Impress the client with your memory and note taking skills. Create a working log of all persons in a department, club, etc., including internal and external acquaintances. You must know all of the people who are in the path of you reaching your desired state: "client loyalty."

An example of how you may meet a CEO might begin with meeting the following persons. You meet someone at the guard gate, followed by a person in the elevator (who happens to be the Director), followed by an introduction to an administrative secretary, and then you may meet the VP while sitting in the lobby waiting on your appointment. No matter what business you are in, you will need to know the key decision makers. You may meet people from multiple departments depending on the situation. Keep your eye on the prize; stay focused and write everything down. Bottom line: you need to find the golden goose!

Take notes on the names of each individual as you will cross their paths again. Remember that luck favors a well prepared person. The running log of departments will give you the ability to visualize how your clients function with other departments. You will know which departments to run to and which department to run from. Yes, there are some places you do not need to go and some people that you do not need to meet. Successful professional, taking good notes will help you with sensing danger. Have a sixth sense for warning signs. Your antennas should always be up; trust them! Over time your collected data will enable you to forecast future client opportunities as well as recapture lost ones. Clients want to see you lead and assist them with forecasting their capital projects. Taking charge of the record keeping process shows you have built the client's confidence by being responsible. Show the client you are happy being the repository for their needed and sometimes not-needed information. Get to know the people you will be working with and help them in their endeavors. You will be walking down the hall and collecting notes from all of your contacts when one of those contacts will say "Have you met Sally? I believe she can help you." Suddenly your path detours and you start to see a steady trail of golden eggs. You will say to yourself, "My notes are paying off." Suddenly, out of nowhere, you see a nest of golden eggs, and you know what that means don't you? You have found the golden goose!

Just think of yourself as the information recycling container! You will one day be thanked for helping their organization win globally. Attention to detail in this area will reap you a bountiful harvest. The more data you have on the people and various departments in an organization; the more they will value you for taking the time to recognize them!

Take good notes! Be a good secretary at all times.

Punctuality!

Professionals all around the world win or lose, make it or miss it, sky rocket or sky plummet due to their ability or inability to respect the client's time! Time is the one thing that no organization wants to squander. Clients who seek professional consultation demand sales professionals who will meet deadlines and exceed expectations. So successful professional, what can you do to create opportunities for you? PLAN!!!

The **PLAN Method** will keep you focused and on time with your clients.

> ➢ **P**- Prepare yourself mind, soul and body (harmony in here will wake your senses).
> ➢ **L**- Listen! (Ask the client what is the best time for a uninterrupted solutions meeting.)
> ➢ **A**- Always be on. (No conversation is an idle one; every conversation counts!)
> ➢ **N**- Never be late (if you want all the marbles, you need to be there!!) There is no excuse!

Preparation is not only about forecasting client historical data. Preparation is about YOU spending the time concentrating on what makes you feel good and what makes you tick. You can easily get so sidetracked with all of the spreadsheets, contacts, and competitors that you lose your dreams, long term goals, significant others and your physical health.

God gave us two ears! We must use them to listen. Our clients need us! We are a very important cog in their respective machines. Before delivering a stellar performance we must first sit down and appropriately write the music together. Yes, together! We must be seen as a value added member of the family who wants them to win. The client has many distractions floating in and out of the office daily. We must be sure that we have the necessary strategy time with the correct audience. Wasted time here can be disastrous. Our record keeping must be organized and our follow up impeccable. If you keep your ears open and your lips sealed your wallet will certainly fill up!

Always be on your "A Game!" You have clients everywhere. People are watching your every move and that is what you want! Success is the result of chance meeting opportunity. Every conversation that you have with another person is a chance for something grand to happen. The locations and situations are as vast as the sky and as numerous as the stars. You can close a million dollar deal in a parking lot, YMCA, concert hall, ballet or restaurant. The opportunities for success are limitless. You can ill afford to not wear your leadership hat and be ready to deliver a solution.

Get to your appointments on time every time! Stay on top of your calendar. The client needs you to help them prioritize tasks and budgets. They need you! Give them the courtesy of getting there prepared or you will lose your chance to a competitor who will be. Never be late to an agreed upon time. Once you gain the top client resource, "time," you must work like a brick mason to complete the project. Brick by brick you must add resources to support your claim as the best solutions specialist. Why is it important to add resources? The time the customer gives you is for one purpose: productivity! Organizations today want thinkers, not followers. Successful professionals like yourself need to challenge clients to think from rooftop levels and to allow you the flexibility to add thinkers to boot. Once you have provided culture changing solutions for a client, you will be thought of first when other opportunities arise.

Can you hear the dinner bell chiming? Come and get it!!

If you get there too late all of the food will be gone!

5

Theme: Present Yourself Professionally

Re-invent yourself.

> "Never stop looking in the mirror.
> You will become who you believe you will become."
> -Robert W. Morris, Sr. (My Uncle)

When you are green you grow and when you are ripe you rot. Organizations are constantly re-structuring departments, products and services in order to attract more customers and improve their brand. Individuals today must re-invent their brand image also to gain a competitive advantage. Successful professional, you must believe that you can change your tomorrow by concentrating on today. The reason why people are slow to greatness is because of a little tiny word called "fear." Fear is a mind killer! You must face it and learn to control it. People go through life with past experiences of failure and allow those negatives to stick with them. Successful professional, let's change the game and "Re-Invent" yourself. You can become your greatest aspiration whether it is a professor, coach, model, actress, race car driver, singer, author, pastor, or cowboy—you name it and it can be attained! Through your spirituality you have an unlimited supply of faith, purpose and destiny.

Let me explain to you what re-invention is in regards to your brand. We all have a uniqueness that makes us who we are. You can, however, add bits and pieces of someone else's profession and their style to better distinguish *you*. Let's say you want to distinguish your brand menu. You may want to investigate someone who you think is distinctive and possibly change a few pieces of your wardrobe to make yourself stand out as well. You do not have to go overboard but adding a little flair will change the way you are perceived and may give you an advantage. What if you added a little Ralph Lauren to your repertoire? Depending on your profession you could add significant points to your brand by changing your attire to a more appropriate look. Doing some research on how Ralph Lauren became a global fashion icon would also give you a behind the scenes look at his branding and how you can have the same success. Adding new elements to your life will definitely affect you and the people around you positively. Re-inventing yourself will cause your clients to re-invent themselves also. Your passion to serve them accompanied by your passion to reach your personal goals will give you superhero-like attributes.

Clients, family and friends all notice everything about you and feed off of your enthusiasm. If you are a lady who is shy or you feel uncomfortable about your physical attributes try adding a little Lynda Carter. Yes, turn into Wonder Woman when you get a chance. That's right! Re-invent yourself by hitting the gym, taming your diet, and getting a monthly massage and spa. Clients want and need people with larger than life auras around them. The superhero that you choose to emulate wears their brand as a costume. Successful professional, you must also change your branding costume. Your dress code is a key component in the re-invention cycle. The new uniform represents the new you!

Here are my top re-invention techniques:

> **Confidently change your style:** Self-fulfilling prophecy states: You become who you believe you will become. Become Sophia Lauren, Wonder Woman, Jack Welch, Lee Iacocca, Emeril Lagasse or whomever you admire. Just add a little of your inspiration's style and the transformation will begin.

> **Get active in your community:** Visibility in helping improve the lives of others will re-invent your service to a

cause. Increase your community presence. Make some new acquaintances.

> **Find a good workout partner:** Your body can be re-invented. You can work off the pounds and refine your shape. The key to having a better looking body is consistency. Find a partner who will stick to the regimen with you. The more the merrier!

> **Get some new frames:** If you wear glasses, please invest in some stylish eyewear! Nice frames add a lot of charm to your facial features.

> **Find a good church home:** Spiritual stability will help you stay grounded and will provide direction. The people that will become a second family to you will support your re-invention efforts without prejudice. Your brand will reach higher heights as they will network for you.

Successful professional, remember that everyone can re-write the script of their life and become a new person. The person looking back at you in the mirror is a true winner. The preceding techniques will give you the confidence to re-invent yourself and start a new chapter.

When they see you at your next high school reunion, they will all say "Wow"!!

Your dress represents you, your family, your organization and your customer.

Have you ever noticed the confidence that emanates from people that are well dressed? Think about the lady who walks in the room with the beautiful dress, stunning smile and warm personality. Envision the gentleman with the nice slacks, fitted jacket, pleasant smell and immaculate grooming. I am certain that you have noticed either of these two people at some point. Successful professional, as you re-invent yourself update your wardrobe and if necessary your hairstyle for a competitive advantage. Your dress code is a clear indicator of how you feel about yourself, your family and your organization.

Customers view a well-dressed professional as a person who shows pride in themselves. I have some very fond memories about two very distinctive people with whom I worked early in my career.

The first person that I truly admire for how she presented herself at work was Tamera Fox. Tamera was an account manager at the time and was one of the few women who worked in Industrial Distribution in the late 80's. Tamera would walk into the branch with flair, confidence and charisma. The ladies and gentleman in the branch all admired how she took on the heavy and light manufacturing clients in Richmond, Virginia. The clear distinction Tamera had over her competition stemmed from the facts that she knew all of the features and benefits of the organization and the fashion style she presented was elegant and tailored. Tamera always came to work like she was walking down the runway of a fashion show. Make no mistake—we all knew she was in the building as she wore her perfume thick. I can recall a good friend of mine named Dale Barnett who always alerted the team when Tamera walked in the building. Dale would say "Mama is in the building; hallelujah!" We all respected Tamera because of the attention to detail she demanded for herself and that polish carried over onto others. Tamera set a standard for me for how women should present themselves at work. Successful professional, remember you are always interviewing and people are always watching you.

The second person that I have admired for his workplace fashion presentation was a former manager named Jeff W. of Cary, North Carolina. I can say, without a doubt, Jeff dressed like a model for a JoS A. Bank Commercial! Jeff was the manager that gave me one of the best opportunities of my career, but what really impressed me about Jeff was his attention to detail. The style that Jeff had, in my opinion, was vintage 60's. I never saw Jeff with a wrinkled shirt or slacks; his shoes were always shined and matched his belt. Jeff infused the same polish into the future leaders that he managed. The expectation that Jeff had of all the facilities that he managed was to operate a first class business with no exceptions or excuses! I remember a particular manager who was present at one of our regional break out meetings in the summer and he was not wearing a tee shirt. Opting not to wear a tee shirt is OK, provided you do not have heavy perspiration issues. Jeff had one of the liveliest personalities and was super fun to be around. Jeff opened the meeting that day and said "We need to get that guy a damn tee shirt! If he is sweating like this now, what will that look like in front of our customers?" Everyone in the room busted out in laughter. Jeff was making fun but was very serious at the same time. We must hold our outward appearance in high standards as it is one the first things a person notices and will likely judge you on. The dress code that you exhibit will be seen by all and it will shape how they feel about your ability to represent them. Keep pushing the Cary Grant/Coco Chanel envelope!

Here are my fashion re-invention tips:

> **Subscribe to a fashion magazine:**
> Let the fashion design experts keep you in the loop on seasonal changes. Cut out the styles you like and create your own portfolio of fashion.

> **Find a good tailor:**
> Your tailor is a clothes fitting genius! Without a good tailor you will never maximize the look you want to achieve. They know what to take in and what to take out!

> **Invest quarterly in building your fashion wardrobe:**
> Purchase an article once a month. Remember that you are a reflection of your organization to a lot of people so look good where ever you go! Opportunities are found in various community and social events. Do not let the fashion police put you in jail.

> **Wear your new "you" with confidence:**
> You make the clothes; the clothes do not make you! Own the catwalk and showcase your style.
> The first step in making a million bucks is to look like a million bucks!

Look marvelous!

One White Shirt.

When you look good you feel good! Looking your best will give you an opportunity to outshine the rest. Successful professional, you have only 2 minutes and 2 seconds to make a good first impression. Why leave that 2 and 2 to chance? You are first class! Controlling your image is a must in delivering a rock solid first impression. Let me tell you about my great, great aunt, Mrs. Maggie Moore Robinson. My aunt "Sis", as she was fondly called, taught one of the greatest lessons in my life about the necessity to look your best.

The year was 1989 when I was looking through the Richmond Times Dispatch classified section hoping to find a job. It was my first year of college and I wanted to find a job that was related to accounting. Well, there were not many opportunities for accounting clerks. The job market was filled with laborers, restaurant cooks and warehousemen. I had been circling job opportunities all over the classified ads every day that summer but none showed any interest. One company, however, had in very bold print the starting salary wage of $7.15 to work in the warehouse. I circled that one but was hesitant because it was a warehouse job. My aunt watched me every day as I got prepared to go job hunting and she always asked, "Have you checked out that warehouse job?" I replied "I am not going to get all dirty working in a warehouse!" I will never forget the reply that my aunt Sis made: "Oh yeah, you are going to do something!" My aunt was an incredible pastor of our small family church. The next comment from her was "You sometimes can't see what God has in store for you!" My aunt Sis operated on a very high level of spiritual passion. I took heed and proceeded to take the two hour bus trip to Industrial Distributors. What is so funny, as I look back at traveling to this job, is that I was only thirty minutes away via automobile transportation. I did not have a car at the time so the GRTC (Greater Richmond Transit Company) bus line was how I got there. The trek was a long 2 and a half hours both ways.

I will never forget Industrial Distributors located in Richmond, Virginia. I walked into the showroom and saw many dynamic building products. I asked to speak with the general manager but he was not in. Ironically, the assistant general manager was in and his name was Mr. James Johnson. I remember James as a very polished Industrial Supply Manager. James sat at a small desk outside of the office of the General Manager. He reared back in his chair and said to me in front of everyone in the office, "What do you have to offer, young man?" I responded by saying "I am the person you need for an inside customer service position." James quickly informed me that the firm was not hiring for that position. I replied "Well thanks anyway", shook Mr. Johnson's hand, and proceeded to exit the facility.

It was during the long walk to the bus stop when the reality set in that I did not have a job. I would have to face my aunt Sis in two hours. I was contemplating the most compelling story I could tell her. My aunt Sis was born in 1913 in Patulous County, North Carolina and was the youngest daughter of 16 children; very petite, and very fiery. As soon as I walked in the kitchen she asked "How did everything go at Industrial Distributors?" My head was down and I gave her the answer "I did not take the job because I wanted to work in customer service." "What!" she replied and started swinging the dishtowel every which a way. Man was she hot! Aunt Sis shouted "You had better beg for that job and don't come back unless you have it!" You talk about pressure of the worst kind. So off I went back on the bus for 2 and a half more hours.

Successful professional, remember your persistence accompanied by your support system's motivation can help you move mountains. James Johnson was standing at the counter when I walked back in. James had a snicker and smile on his face when we made eye contact. James's remark was "What do you want now?" My reply was "Sir, I need that job today or I will not be able to go home." He laughed!!! "OK, then! Mr. Goode, unload that 52 foot trailer at dock number 2." I started to backpedal immediately. "I do not have a change of clothes with me," I said. Mr. Johnson replied: "Unload it now or forget it!" All I could think about was how dirty my "White Shirt" was going to be after unloading that trailer. So I went Geronimo and jumped right in! I made it back to my aunt's house and she asked "Where in the world have you been? Look at you!" My reply: "I have been working at my new job." My aunt was so excited! She said "Take off those dirty clothes and I will wash them and put them on the line for you. You must look your best every day! We will keep your shirt looking nice until you get your first pay check."

So every day for two weeks my "White Shirt" was cleaned and starched by hand. The guys in the warehouse used to kid me by saying "Why does that little guy come to a warehouse in a white shirt every day?" My reply was short and sweet: "I will be passing out your check stubs one day." My opportunities came very quickly from that point forward and I of course passed out many check stubs! I can honestly say that because of my attitude I have been able to strive for more than the status quo. Believing that there was a better opportunity for me pushed me to find it. Just think! If I had just settled for the job that was posted, I may not have had an opportunity to grow into other areas of the organization. You must show that you are polished in order for people to treat you with polish.

Success in any job will begin with how much pride you have in your appearance each day—no exceptions! People will label you based on how well you label yourself. Successful professional do not leave your appearance to chance. I just love "White Shirts!"

"Now go back and get that job!"
Maggie Moore Robinson, "Aunt Sis" 1913-1992

Great tips for first impressions:

➤ Smile! Whiten your teeth (take care of your choppers).
➤ Clip and clean your nails (no discussion!)
➤ Smell good! (That's right, meet people at their noses! The WOW factor.)
➤ Never wear a wrinkled shirt (pay the 99 cents at the cleaners).
➤ Do not be afraid to be the most "beautiful" woman in the room or the most "handsome" man in the room (own the catwalk).
➤ Treat yourself to a nice handbag or briefcase (your tote says a lot about you).

➤ Be mindful of your shoes. Pay more for comfort and quality. (Take care of your footwear, as it will keep your feet comfortable and improve back ergonomics).

➤ Say "good morning", "good afternoon" and "good evening" (sincere salutations are important).

➤ Shake hands firmly! (You can lose the deal before you sit down at the table!)

➤ Invite a client to a picnic lunch (professional charm and etiquette goes a long way).

➤ Keep your automobile clean on the inside at all times! (No exceptions.)

Investing in your outward appearance will create an incredible aura about you. Believing in you is step number one and step number two is doing something about it.

Take complete charge of your first impressions.
Never leave it to chance.

Presentation is everything.

Can you remember the last formal dinner that you attended? I am sure you can visualize the 5 star resort that just sent you to a sensory bliss. I am sure you felt the quality and professionalism of each person who served you. You know what I am talking about! It is called "presentation!" There are times when you can just *feel* the polish. Organizations want to partner with polished people. Clients who win are the clients who never take for granted the intricate details of presentation. Successful professionals today can attain superior market share by taking the necessary steps to deliver polish to all acquaintances.

Everyone you meet is going through some sort of challenge. We must take the road less traveled and deliver a great presentation every time. Your presentation will leave a lasting impression on your clients. Lead with character and close with integrity! You want to differentiate yourself from the competition by being the best person you can be. Here are some polish points that clients carefully look for from a stellar successful professional.

Top "Polish Point" Tips:

> **Paper:** Use quality paper for all formal proposals! Please do not use your standard printer to produce top line presentations as it will look cheap. Just think how you would feel to receive $250,000 on lackluster paper quality. Your champion may have to present your proposal to their manager! (If your work is sloppy, then they might look sloppy.)

> **Dress Code:** Always! Always! Always! Impress the client by looking your best. Looking average will subliminally make your client feel that you do not have on your thinking cap. Look like a million bucks and you may receive an opportunity for a million bucks.

> **Email:** Oh Boy! Presentation must be in the forefront of your mind when sending emails. Successful professional, remember that what you write and how you write speaks volumes about your manners, grammar, and critical thinking skills. Know your audience! Read your email twice before you send it and if necessary print it out and read it over again just to make sure you did not make any mistakes. Email communication can be the deal breaker!

> **Health:** Invest the time to take care of your body. Clients want champions who look their best inside and outside. Discipline will be needed as power lunches create "power pounds!" Health is the first impression that people label us with before we open our mouths. We can eat better, exercise more, and step up our hygiene to give us a better chance to own the opportunity.

> **Meals:** Yes, lunches matter! Use your budgets wisely. Closing deals with certain meals are definite difference makers. Focus on the client for lunch and they will focus on you!

Meals

"The Hemingway" – Breakfast: select a high end hotel and present your proposal there. You will score huge presentation points for detail. The early bird gets the worm.

"The Lee Iacocca" - "Power Lunch": the power lunch is for vision and long range planning. The power lunch is about you! Do not limit this lunch to clients. Invite your pastor to lunch. Remember, successful professional, that clients want a holistic person who is morally sound.

"The Langston" – Dinner: the ultimate presentation, should flow like poetry. Dinner should be an intimate way of closing the deal. Ambiance will change the mood of your client and will unlock multiple networking corridors. Stay focused at dinner. You are an ambassador of good will.

Presentation can change the game for you. Work tirelessly to create your own polished approach in helping people. You may not think someone notices! Trust me; they do.

White china decorates the chocolate cake and fine silver turns a regular cup of coffee into Breakfast at Tiffany's! Create first class lasting impressions.

6

Theme: Relationships

People do not buy from companies. They buy from you!

"You are a striped, polka-dotted zebra; embrace your uniqueness!"
-Dr. Alberta H. Herron

Do you have a favorite restaurant or store that you visit frequently? Nine times out of ten the warm experience that you had was based on the service of your maître de, associate, or owner. The decisions people make when purchasing a good or service often boils down to the service they receive. In order to appreciate good service you must first learn how to give good service! One of the largest mistakes we can make is underestimating the power of you in assisting people. No matter what area of expertise you are in people will give the opportunity to individuals who put themselves on the line. The fact of the matter is that *you* know the product, service, features, benefits, and advantages. Organizations want long term growth or SCA! Simply put, they want a Sustained Competitive Advantage. A continual stream of success comes to ordinary people who show interest and invest their time in the small things. Solving small challenges is the key to gaining trust on solving larger obstacles. Successful professional, you do not have to drive with your courage and wonderful attitude sitting in the back seat. Drive success to your clients with courage and attitude, riding shotgun, buckled up tight, and with the top down!

Managers today often comment that a person should never allow the organization to take the blame for a miscue at any time. The rationale is that a successful professional would put them in a compromising situation which could hurt the reputation of the organization. Here is what I have found to be more credible: Successful professional, no matter what the situation is, at the end of the day it will be *your* reputation on the line! Help your organization and others grow but at the same time look out for Numero Uno! Make every effort to give 150% to your clients (students, customers, peers, staff etc.) Your clients will notice your broad shoulders and stretched visionary wings as you face stiff competition by delivering detailed proposals. Managers who are engulfed with organizational initiatives and have limited communication with the day to day client often forget the balance.

People do buy from organizations but if you have a Sustained Competitive Advantage it will be the "you" that the client will give the million dollar account to.

Successful professional: Opportunities are attained by people who are on top of these things!

- ➤ People who can interpret large complex projects (Visionary).
- ➤ People who can interpret small tedious projects (Short Range Closer).
- ➤ People who show compassion (Always Giving).
- ➤ People with the tenacity to go the extra mile (Project Completion).
- ➤ People who walk with confidence! (Own the Opportunity).

All of these traits are stored up inside of you! The time is now to unlock them.

Let the "you" loose and show them all you've got!

You are always interviewing.

Interviews, interviews, interviews! Old acquaintances, new acquaintances, and people that somehow crossed your path may all be the gatekeepers of a blessing with your name on it. You may receive your gift in the form of an opportunity, lead, referral, or promotion. Here's the caveat: you will only receive it after a successful interview with them. Yes, you are always on the hot seat because the people you meet will always try to verify your character and motives. Every person you meet is a CEO of some sort. Your character is who you are when no one else is looking. Guess what? Somebody is looking! The nurses, physicians, church members, VPs, CEOs, receptionists, coaches, principals, janitors, secretaries, and engineers are all dissecting your character. Your public wants to know what you are really about on the inside and whether or not you really want to help them grow. Let attitude and commitment be your guide and engage yourself in stellar dialogue. Make sure everyone understands your brand, what you stand for, who you work for, and how you have the tools to help them. Remember it is not what you say about yourself that makes you great; it is what other people say about you that makes you great!

Let me tell you about a very unique client; his name is Danny Taylor. Working in Industrial Distribution I noticed that my champions all possessed great interviewing skills. My first endeavor was with a top notch interviewer at Vulcan Materials. Danny is one of the best people that I have had the fortune to meet in Winston-Salem, North Carolina. My first week on the job was filled with cold calls so I had to explore the ins and outs of my 75 new clients. I will never forget the initial interview with Danny and everyone in Vulcan Materials. Here is the dialogue from my first interview with Danny:

Danny: "Well fellar it is a pleasure to meet you! Where are you from?"(**Probing question**)
Antwain: "Danny, likewise! I am your new Account Manager and a native of Richmond, Virginia."

Danny: "How are you going to help Vulcan grow our business?" (**Character/action question**)
Antwain: "I need your help in understanding your business first and afterwards we will together formulate a solution."
Danny: "Antwain, you are one fired up individual! Today I will give you a shot!"(**Validate character**)
Antwain: "Danny, I will work hard to better your organization. Can you introduce me to heads of your departments today? I am ready!"
Danny: "You have a great attitude; let me help you!"(**Validate work ethic**)

The next round of interviews for me within Vulcan was with Carrie Myers and Chris Ashley. These two dynamic ladies became more than executive mentors; they were God-delivered angels. Carrie and Chris pushed me farther than I could imagine on how to service others and to keep trying! Successful professionals, take your referrals from your interviews very seriously. People that believe in you have their reputation on the line. Right after my interviews with Carrie Myers she introduced me to Pete Roberts who at the time was the DPL (short for Division Procurement Leader). Remember with every successful interview the pressure to deliver will mount up! The escalation is due to all of the people who have co-signed for your work ethic. Well, Pete Roberts to me was something like the Godfather! Pete was polished, sincere and direct about what type of service he wanted from me and for his organization. So, with both barrels staring me down I did what any new Account Executive would do: I said, "Pete, I have the energy to make it happen. I am ready to meet the president of Vulcan today!"

The age old statement "be careful what you wish for" suddenly applied to me just that quickly. Pete said, "Antwain you are at the Mid-East Corporate office; let me ring Hal or Gray and see if they can meet with you!" Just then I started to feel the sweat beads rolling off my neck; my face was hot and my eyes were the size of golf balls. Pete picked up the phone and called Hal Cox, the Vice President of the Mid East Division. I had no preparation for this meeting with Hal but all I wanted to do was to introduce my character, integrity, polish and 15+ years of experience with being a leader for my organization. Hal met with me and gave me a whopping eight minutes. Hal, to my surprise, later was in sales for Vulcan at one point. I am certain he had sympathy for me that day. Hal gave me the fastest and most concise instruction on how to service his team of leaders. See, with Pete's recommendation Hal gave me a shot. I tell you the truth: Vulcan showed me something so incredibly great that day! Vulcan's culture is one in which its leaders intimately know their leaders and they build and promote external leaders also.

Here are some tips to consider for your formal and informal interviews:

- ➢ Have a 30 second commercial about yourself (it's halftime at the Super Bowl every day).
- ➢ Create a clear statement of how you can help someone else. (What are your gifts?)
- ➢ Remember everyone you meet is going through a challenge. (You can enlighten their life.)
- ➢ Be confident! (Focus your attitude on the client.)
- ➢ Smile often (to have a friend you must show yourself as friendly).
- ➢ Read the front page of the Wall Street Journal daily (deliver current global information).
- ➢ Ask for a referral (Deliver, Execute and Serve).
- ➢ If you do not ask, you do not get! (Nothing else said.)
- ➢ Meet the CEO today! (What do you have to lose?) Have some GUTS!

The all-important interview: do not take it lightly; instead embrace the chance to meet the person who will shape your life…

…or better yet, the life you will shape by someone meeting you!

Get comfortable with meeting people.

Problems, conflicts, disasters and catastrophes—what do all of these things have in common? They all have people that are begging for a successful professional, like you, to lift them from despair and render them a victory! People that receive your service will reward you for value, intuitiveness, punctuality and character. You are a battle winner! So, how do you continue making successes day in and day out? You don't! The people that you serve will help you. What you have to do is to get comfy with meeting people. People want you! I said it. People need you! I said that, too. People want and need you to diagnose and prescribe solutions that help them not be afraid of the people they work for or people they work with.

Successful professional you must shift the mindset and cast off the disbelief that people need to meet you. You have no need to be afraid of meeting people as there is someone out there who needs your abilities to help them solve a problem. It is the "you" that makes the difference; it is the "you" that organizations will invest in as a personal consultant to their respective business. Do you know what you get when people invest in you? You get the "magical pot of gold"—client loyalty! To the people that are reading this book and are afraid of people; you cannot live this life alone thinking that you are the all-knowing Wizard of Oz! You could easily miss the many blessings God wishes to bestow on you through other people. In order to get comfortable with meeting new people you must start by being thankful for what God has created you to be! Your uniqueness is the seed that will grow into strong lifelong relationships.

When was the last time you looked in the mirror and said, "Thank you God for me"?

Please look at my top 7 tips to help you get more comfortable with new relationships:

- To make a friend, be friendly (open up).
- Your gaze (successful eye contact shows sincerity).
- Look like a million bucks (opportunities can knock anywhere and at any time).
- Know current events (join the Chamber of Commerce—know what is going on in town).
- Do your homework. (If you do not know your customer, please Google them.)
- Establish common ground (engage in dialogue that is mutually beneficial).
- Compliments (give a compliment; it always stirs dialogue).

Please invest the time in preparing "you" to meet someone new! The encounters you make today will open up your doors for rewards tomorrow. Do not take anyone for granted! You need to meet people from all over the globe to round off your corners and add intricate detail to you character.

Get ready for a tidal wave of new contacts...

Surf's up!

Success is built person by person.

"A candle's light is faint, but where there is total darkness it can
be seen from miles away."
Antwain T. Goode

The most rewarding achievements in life begin with people. Successful relationships are forged by the establishment of trust, loyalty and commitment! Investing constructive time with the people around you who are goal focused will increase your chances to own an opportunity. Who do you know? We can live in a city all of our lives and never invest in new relationships. Have you ever met people who relocate and they somehow build relationships all over the city? People that relocate have to rely on others to help them figure it out. You got it! They are humble enough to ask and people are receptive to their situation and help them get there. You must use your pleasantries! "Good mornings", "hellos", and warm smiles all play a significant part in forging relationships. Every person you meet is going through something. So why not become the difference maker to help them grow? Take a chance and meet someone new; join that women's league, YMCA basketball league, or chess club. You are one person away from success!

People all around you will see your light shining. Your flame must brighten the day of everyone you meet. No excuses. Waking up in the morning is a blessing. Today is the "Great Day" and you must be prepared to receive every opportunity deserving of you. What I have found out in life is that you have more than one brother, sister, uncle, aunt, mother or father. The Lord works very mysteriously! The anointing that God has cloaked over your life will attract the personalities that will take you in as one of their own. I want you to be aggressive about making life connections. There are people in the world that you need to meet and people in the world who need to meet you. Your success in your life will be measured by the people that you touch, the people that touch you and your service to others. You got it! Brick by brick networking will be the tunnel that your productivity will flow through.

Add a friend today!

Your customers want you to win!

Clients today want to be inspired and uplifted. Unleashing productivity within you will cause others to open up and share their gifts and talents. The standard requirements of service, quality, price and availability are the same for most organizations. The key differentiator between you and your competition may be the inspirational element! When you are enjoying preferred positioning with your client base, remember to give "hope!" Your customers have real feelings and they may not show them to you initially. Once people see your consistent hard work and your ability to solve problems, they will then allow you to see their personal side. Now, do not take this for granted! Remember the attitude building blocks in chapter two: Love, Giving, Humility, Hunger, Mission and Desire. Have your attitude revved up for the challenge.

Successful professional, the hope that you will bring to people that you meet will help you to forge amazing relationships. The customer will turn into a client, and from a client into a friend. Organizational culture can be changed when people truly partner with other people to solve complex issues for mutual benefit. As stated before, the key to handling negative situations is to "be prepared." You will face some of your toughest opposition when your friendships hit a speed bump and then you may have a hot tempered customer on your hands. Successful professional, do not hit the panic button; instead rely on your "sticktoitness". Yes, stick-to-it-ness! Stick to the values, problem solving abilities, and all of the stuff that made you the person of choice for that organization. Know that you have been included in their corporate family and remind them of the battles you have won together. Align new resources to help redeem any lost confidence. The due diligence you have shown working on the tougher projects will shield you from many fiery darts. And at the end of the day, your customer, client and friend will recommend you and your talents to everyone they meet. Successful professional, you do not have to fight the entire battle alone. Your clients want you to win and will help you get there!

Always give "hope" and "hope" will be given unto you.

7

Theme: Opportunities

Embracing opportunities!

"Be careful not to talk too loud as
the faint opportunity knocks will not be heard."
-Antwain T. Goode

Who's that knocking at the door? I think I heard someone knocking. Have you ever had a knock on the door, but were hesitant to open it?? Successful professionals, there will be situations in your lives in which you will feel that someone or something is attempting to get your attention. Prepare yourself to be sensitive to your inner feelings! Opportunities are wonderful, but first you must hear them rap on the door and meet them head on. The more you brand yourself with energy, attitude, passion, and power the more diverse opportunities will befall you. Clients are anyone you come into contact with. Successful professional, never, and I mean *never* treat anyone as if they are not on your level of equal intelligence. Your best and most fulfilling opportunities will blindside you as they will come to you as warm sunrays. "Good professionals" become "great professionals" when opportunity and chance meet.

Opportunity and chance make the perfect storm for growing top line revenue! You must ride this tidal wave that will take you and your family to the next level. Opportunities are sometimes loud and complex projects which are very visible, while others have no pulse and seem dormant. I can tell you that sometimes all an opportunity needs is a jolt of lightning and that faint pulse will turn into a 20 million dollar Frankenstein.

It's alive!!!

Own the Opportunity! Work your butt off.

So! We now have an opportunity; what in the devil are we going to do with it? You have your eye on the ball and you recognize it is a fastball coming straight down the middle. Get ready to hit it over the wall for a grand slam! The next step after recognizing an opportunity is figuring out how to own the opportunity. When some competitor spots you with a golden egg, chances are they will want one, and those competitors are greedy. The competition today does not just want your egg. They want the whole goose!

The strategy for owning the opportunity lies with a life lesson given to me by my uncle Robert Morris. He would always say to me: "Ann," (short for Antwain), "Work your butt off!" Clients that give you an opportunity not only trust in you but know you will deliver results that will grow their business. Clients give you opportunities because they want "you!" Yes "you!" The opportunity is the green light to translate the client's vision into quantifiable results. Work your butt off and you will achieve those results.

People often get overly excited when the opportunity knocks. You must be a professional at all times. Take your time to thoroughly analyze the client's desired state and use the opportunity to plant seeds for the future. One of my favorite graduate professors from High Point University was Dr. David Little. Dr. Little was my mentor for Strategic Operations and Global Supply Chain Management. Dr. Little drilled me constantly with the theory of SCA. Successful professional, you do not want to win just one championship; you want a Sustained Competitive Advantage. In other words: "A dynasty!" The one-time, large-hit outliers will fade away; however, the hard work of building consistent victories will enhance your brand as a premier problem solving expert! I owe so much to Uncle Robert for stressing the importance of developing a solid work ethic and to Dr. Little for his Ali/Frazier knockout lectures!

It's your opportunity. You earned it!

The successful people in our lives that we idolize all show great persistence through a six letter word called "effort." Your talents and abilities will aid you in unlocking more productivity within yourself; but without effort you will be walking in quicksand.

The year was 1994 and I was working as an Onsite Integration team member at Allied Signal Honeywell in Chester, Virginia. I have always been very ambitious about the opportunity to lead and to be a part of large corporate strategies. Well, opportunity and chance met for me when the position of On Site Manager opened up. People complain every day about receiving a fair shake: "no one will help them" or (the most famous line): "he/she was on the fast track." The truth is, you can get a next at bat if you show some "effort!" I have been very fortunate to have worked for some great managers, all of whom shared the same philosophy: "Outwork the competition." Competing for an upper management position will change the way you see yourself, your peers and your clients.

I will never forget the day before my big interview as I spent it with two very close friends: Kevin Earley and Jay Straughan. I knew that I had a big day ahead of me and that I needed to associate myself with the right support group. Kevin arranged for us to meet at one of the best restaurants in Richmond for baked spaghetti: Jimmy the Greek on W. Broad Street. While at dinner, Jay (who is one bear of a man, bald on top and a second degree black belt) started the conversation with, "Twain, what are you trying to go for now?" My reply was, "On Site Manager." Jay was from upper Mechanicsville, had a distinctly long accent and looked like Paul Bunyan. What I loved about Jay was his sincerity in friendship and open candor. The big man always had a way to push his friends whether they liked it or not. Jay followed up that comment by saying, "Antwain you have worked hard in every position that you have ever had so own this opportunity as well!" Sometimes the way Jay looked at you, one would have to wonder, if you did not do it, would Bruce Lee come out of him and chop you on top of your head?

Kevin—my best friend in the world—always positioned God's influence over the lives of people before any selfish plans of their own. Kevin's motto has always been "It's not about you but about the God that lives in you." Kevin informed me that "you have an opportunity so make the most out of it." Mayors do not become mayors overnight, but do so opportunity by opportunity, and you are no different. Successful professional, the people you choose for your support system will make a difference in the opportunities that you capture! The assurance that was drilled into me that night gave me the confidence to hone all of my skill sets for my interview.

The next day I was so focused and determined to win the position. My interview was with three very unique leaders whom I respected for their rigorous leadership styles. Ron and David had over 25 years of service at the time and Tim was in senior leadership. I was 25 years of age so you can imagine the pressure; however because of the pep talk from my support system I felt that I had 25 years on my side as well. The question was asked by the panel, "What can you do to motivate the staff and increase their productivity for the client?" My reply was "I will motivate the staff by working hard to support their dreams and aspirations; by supporting their goals the team will help the client with theirs!" Two weeks later I was offered the job.

Successful professional, I tell you about this life altering experience because you have to believe you can "compete and win!" You must rally your value added support team and resources to your camp and let them give you the edge to conquer your fears. The opportunities that you will pursue will require you to be mentally tough. Take destiny into your own hands.

Own the opportunity!

If the stove is hot, do not touch it!

Kenny Rogers said it plainly, "You got to know when to hold 'em and when to fold 'em, know when to walk away and know when to RUN." There is a time and a place for everything and we must have our antennas up at all times. Do you remember how hot it got in the kitchen when your mom, grandma or your aunts would be cooking? They would always be shouting out when children were in the vicinity to get out of the kitchen as the pots on the stove are hot and the oven is smoking. Well guess what? The same rule applies to us in being great in our respective organizations. The opportunities that we encounter are all linked to people. The people/opportunities that you touch may be the flame that will burn you! Successful professional, you must listen to your gut feelings when you anticipate danger or suspect you are meeting someone who is lacking character. Because you are unleashing leadership, confidence, and hope some people will resent you and try to shut you down. Be encouraged as not everyone in the world will support you; but hold steady to the favor that God has over you.

I remember one client in particular whom I never really trusted. There are some people that you will meet that will test you, your family, your organization and everything else that exudes good in your life. The client was in a high profile position and from the first time I met this gentlemen I just had a gut feeling that he had other motives. The sneer that he gave me during one of my business reviews (which we performed to show how we could deliver select resources to help their business) was apparent immediately. This particular person changed in the boardroom immediately from a person who I thought had some level of concern for me to a person who did not care about me or anything to which I belonged. Because of my tenure and coaching from some extremely tough managers, I knew from the first day to always take the high road with any customer. The golden rule should always be in effect no matter what the opposition. I was determined to meet the challenge with energy, attitude, passion and power!

The vibe from this particular client was always the same: "I'm the big client and the world revolves around me." Well, I'll tell you the truth: this puny, beanie eyed fellow was not the top dog, but had built a reputation over the years as a junk yard dog. He was just a "hot stove!" He was a gate keeper and wanted attention. So what did I do? I gave him more attention. Successful professional, you are in the people business not the battle business. The client of course was happy temporarily because of the added attention but as soon as an opportunity presented itself he would go back to being a "hot stove." So what should you do when you have one of these on your hands? Get the hell out of the kitchen!!!

You are an incredible person who has incredible talents and abilities. The fact that you are showing character, valor, service, grit and compassion to someone who does not acknowledge your effort should not go unnoticed! There are people in this world who take great pleasure in knocking people down so when you see a "hot stove" be cautious. The battle will be won for you with intervention and truth from the mouths of others that see your effort! Not all opportunities, no matter how sweet they might look, are for you. Carefully analyze the scenario that will reward you for your leadership, brand, time and problem solving abilities. So what was the final outcome for me with this hot stove of a character? What did I do to battle the heat? You guessed it! Nothing!

I did not have to do a thing! The Lord fought that battle for me the through the people of that entire organization. You will be amazed at the number of people who recognize true character and hard work. You construct allies every day with "Thank you's", "Hello's", "How are you doing's", "Good morning's" or just a simple smile. People see your light and lean over for you to help theirs ignite. That situation gave me tremendous confidence to face any hothead. Remember the easiest way to combat the hot stove personality is to let that person stay hot all by themselves. Isolation! People in their own organization will begin to see their poor character and jealous motives. Typically those people have high blood pressure and stay at the doctor's office.

Successful professional, don't be fooled; some opportunities are not worth it.

Here are some steps to take to avoid that "hot stove"!

➢ Gut awareness (a person's character is felt, and then seen. Trust your intuition!)
➢ Twice fooled (you touched the stove! It's Hot. Why touch it again?) Back away!
➢ Network higher and wider (9 times out of 10 they are not the top wolf. Validate their status!)
➢ Stay away (you have great health. Let them have the heart attack!) Sorry I have call this one like it is.
➢ Pray for them (OK, I felt guilty about them having a heart attack).

Successful professional, know that you are a unique and unrepeatable miracle of God.

You are valuable to so many people and you have a light that shines bright.

Do not let anyone blow out your candle!

If you want it, go get it!

There is gold in them there hills. Millionaires are made every 11 seconds. Successful professional, you should take 11 seconds and think of that thing that you are good at that totally makes you happy. Whatever just popped up in your mind is your Million! The success that you want to attain is linked to the perseverance you have to capture your goal. Be relentless in your quest to be fulfilled mentally and physically. The awesome talents and abilities that we have mean nothing unless they are used to help our families and strengthen our communities. You must have "fire in the belly" determination to make your dreams a reality. Who says you cannot have the best of both worlds? You can win mental and physical championships!

Ok! Here is golden nugget that will help you get your "it." Successful professional, one of the best weapons to capture new ground for your life is to "outwork the competition" internally and externally. Cast the negativity, regret and past failures out of the window! It is time for you to boldly take the lion's share of opportunities. Your heroes/heroines all did it, and so can you. So many traps are set for those people who squander time. People that are not pushing the envelope for personal victory have limited intuition for sensing danger. Just like a bear trap lying under a pile of leaves, the complacency will set your mind on autopilot and the once safe path will be an unanticipated snare!

There are people out there who say "There are not enough hours in a day, not enough products to sell, or not enough solutions to present to help you close the gap and gain superior market share." My mental response has always been "You have no idea of your vast array of blessings and favor that God has over your life." The ultimate caveat! Stop worrying and "Go get it!"

The determined have spikes on their heels that allow them to climb the highest mountain. Use your pick ax of character to pull you up if you begin to slip. The temperature can be negative 20 degrees but you are wearing a very warm integrity parka! What I am saying to you, successful professional, is that you are well equipped to capture your dreams, so unlock your imagination and climb like hell toward your destination. You will win as true effort is always rewarded. Passion fuels your character and prepares you for greatness.

Time is limited; so start your trek on Mount Successful today!

Here are my top mountain climbing techniques:

➢ **Focus** ("Fire in the belly" determination is a must.)
➢ **Pursuit** (use your talents and imagination to help you boldly take new market share).
➢ **Dream big** (million dollar opportunities happen every day; you are closer than you think).

- ➢ **You are in the game!** (You are never out! You are only out when your fire goes out.)
- ➢ **Look back** (halfway up the mountain, look back for perspective and new confidence).
- ➢ **Take a breath** (climbing is hard work; rest up! OK, that's enough. Now get up that hill!)

Bottom line: If you want millions you must have the determination to attain millions.

> "Don't be afraid to fail. Embrace it, learn from it and move
> forward. After all, failure is the starting line to success!"
> -Dale Shoop, The manager who taught me
> how to coach, by allowing me to fail!

The world is your oyster. If you want it, go and get it!

8

Theme: Overcoming Conflict

Paint a rainy day!

"Enjoy the rain as each rain drop is a blessing from heaven.
Collect the rewards today!"
-Antwain T. Goode

Life is not perfect! Starting in elementary school we are taught to draw a house with two windows, a door, a tree and a sun in the left hand corner. The truth is, we should have also been taught to draw a rainy day. Successful professional, rainy days are very important. People often show saddened or somber emotions when they see rain outside. You need to resist those feelings and consider yourself fortunate to see and experience those rain drops. What rain really means is that you have your client all to yourself. The competition will hopefully be inside their office or have called in sick because they were afraid of a few raindrops. Remember that the postman always delivers the mail no matter what the weather. You must have the same mindset when you face situations that are challenging. Those challenges are like rain. Yes, you will hear the thunder of health related issues and see the lightning of economic downturns. You must have the mindset that you will be the recipient of "Positive Rain" vs. "Negative Rain."

The positive rain that you want to experience is that of customer loyalty, customer valued leadership, favored positioning, and strong brand image. Successful professional, turn your umbrella upside down! You have invested the right time and resources to serve others, so be excited about collecting your rewards. Clients that give you favored positioning will reward you with gigantic opportunities. The pennies will rain down on you as you have generated so many visionary solutions.

The negative rain is where you will need to hold your umbrella by the handle! Ongoing problems, multiple competitor threats, internal management challenges and family crises will disturb your confidence and distract you. "Positive" and "Negative" rain must be dealt with! Prioritize your work life balance accordingly. Your clients trust you and will give strong value to people who invest quality time with their organization. Successful professional, take a look at the following illustration to learn how to hold your umbrella during "Positive or Negative" rain showers.

Positive Rain

#1 Customer Loyalty
The reward for service

#2 Preferred Positioning
The reward for leadership

#3 Strong Brand Image
The reward for attention to detail

#4 Customer Valued Leadership
The reward for your character

Collecting Rewards

Negative Rain

threats crisis   change conflict

Protection

#1 Protection from competitors
Network higher and wider.

#2 Protection from family crisis
Pray! Work together with your
family on multiple teamwork
scenarios.

#3 Protection from manager conflicts
Appreciate the pressures your
manager may be under. Analyze
how you can help with a solution.

#4 Protection from system upgrades
Ride the wave of change.

Here are some tips to keep in mind as you paint a rainy day:

- ➢ **Get out there in it!** (What a great opportunity to throw a "Hail Mary.") Throw the long ball!
- ➢ **Embrace change** (organizations re-invent themselves and so should you). Ride the wave.
- ➢ **Be thankful** (you are so fortunate to be breathing). You are alive; enjoy the showers.
- ➢ **Thunderstorms and lightning strikes are inevitable** (you know they are coming so get prepared!) Create contingency plans with others; remember if your home is unbalanced your professional life will be unbalanced.

Successful professional, you have earned the rewards because you have braved the negative rain storms. Close your opportunities as quickly as possible as they may wash away from the "Negative Rain" and lightning strikes. Preparing for rain will help you identify your competitor's strategies and enable you to revisit lost opportunities.

Paint a Rainy Day!

Anticipate challenges

The calm before the storm, the smoke before the fire, or the roar before the tornado all are indicators that you need to brace yourself. The epic battles that we face every day have similar indicators. Successful professional, you must recognize the many time robbers that will steer you off your carefully planned journey. The first step in getting prepared for those unknowns is to always have your mission statement (your shield) covering you at all times.

In chapter one you created your mission statement. Your internal preamble is not supposed to sit on a wall or just lay aimlessly in a journal; rather it is to be used to anchor your emotions when life's surprises pop up. The sentence you created for spirituality will need to be recited over and over again until you feel its awesome power throughout your entire body. When you are in tune with your feelings and thoughts you may get a glimpse of lurking danger. Remember that the mission statement that you created is tied to some very strong people in your life. Now is the time to revisit those people and talk through your thoughts and feelings about future pitfalls or opportunities. We often wind up taking the long road to a solution because of pride or not wanting to trouble someone. The people that are the most prepared are victorious because they use their RESOURCES! Bottom line: they get HELP!

The gut feelings that we have are valid and should not be ignored. Your clients can see an unprepared person a mile away. Do not fool yourself by thinking that no one notices or is paying attention. You would be far from the truth. Jeff Watts of RJR Tobacco dropped this quote on me like a hammer on a bare foot. Jeff said, "Antwain, luck favors a well prepared person!" I am grateful to Jeff for that large nugget. The more prepared you are the more calm you will be in the event of a catastrophe. Successful professional, be honest with yourself when it comes to preparation. Piss poor preparation promotes piss poor performance, and piss poor performance promotes pain! Have contingency plans for yourself, your spiritual growth, education, finances and your body. Yeah, your body! If you cannot make it to the gym work out in your garage or in a bedroom and curb your diet. Everything is important to you and you have only one body that must be maintained. Do not be afraid of failure. Meet the challenge head on today.

Here are my top tips for anticipating challenges:

> ➤ **Pray for wisdom.** Matthew 7:7:
>   "Ask and it shall be given, seek and ye shall find, knock and the door will be opened."
> ➤ **Write a plan** (preparation begins by having a roadmap).
> ➤ **Mission statement** (use your preamble to shield you from unforeseen danger).
> ➤ **Apply resources** (Call your value added support team.) It is OK to get HELP!

- ➤ **Listen to your gut** (if you feel uneasiness; put the chain lock on the door!)
- ➤ **Contingency planning** (you must have a backup to protect your dreams).

Keep your mission statement shield held up high!

You are blessed and highly favored; stay calm before the storm.

Know the bottom; get the hell up!

"Commitment: it's the difference between those who attain success and those who dream about it."
-Antwain T. Goode

The clouds look very dark outside. Looks like a serious thunderstorm is brewing? My great aunts would become excellent meteorologists in a split second based on dark cloud cover. The same can be said when it comes to businesses. Everything can be going just fine: stock prices are up, profits are high and sales are coming in hand over foot with no letup in sight. Suddenly, the dark clouds of your competition come in, your largest client loses their competitive advantage and your organization downsizes. Successful professional, you see your commissions dwindle, your clients begin to outsource your services, and some of your competitors will be hired.

You begin to experience the 40 days and 40 nights of turmoil and your confidence about yourself and your service stagnates.

While experiencing the low valleys you will feel loneliness, distance, low managerial support and negative peer comments! Remember the winners in life are the people who are the most persistent and most determined. The never quit, never die attitude is the resting place for overachievers. OK! Let's discuss the nuts and bolts of experiencing rock bottom. The relevant question for people that are in the pit is "How do you get out?" I remember in the spring of 2006, I had just completed one of my best sales years when I was hit with an enormous goal. No matter what your profession, you can and will be asked to hit a target that is unimaginable. So do not cry about it; just dig in your heels and give it your best. Gut checks, reality checks, attitude checks and the possibility of no family time did not sit well with me. My passion to deliver first class solutions was put to the test. I am a competitor who loves a challenge. My clients that year received above and beyond while my goal target held me hostage. I was in need of a spark to charge my emotions and put me back in the driver's seat.

So what did I do to get out? Nothing! It is what others did that pulled me out. Successful professional, remember that when you give it your all to help others, they will rally to you during your hour of trial and need. People were the key element that made me successful in 2006. My extensive network of dynamic, spirited people cheered me back up the ladder. Serving others wholeheartedly pays enormous dividends way down the winding road. Successful professional, just like clockwork you will be rocketed into first place. Your inner voice speaks quietly; just listen! The commotions that large challenges bring often impede our creative thoughts. I am certain that it is then, when your inner voice will give you pertinent instruction on who will assist you on your next move. Be ever mindful that you have invested precious time with your clients and they want you to win! Communicate with them that you are in despair and step back and let them pull you out. Clients see your agony and pain and will introduce you to new opportunities. The bottom of the pit is a cold place, so don't just sit there and freeze to death. Get the creative juices in your mind flowing and build mental muscle by performing brain push-ups.

One major agenda item that must be dealt with while in the pit is the pit fall. Get a grasp on what hurdle tripped you up and caused you to fall in the pit in the first place. What initiative, family challenge, competitive threat or, most importantly, lacking resource caused the event to happen? You must know your surroundings at all times and stay on the lookout for life's booby traps. Finally, the last and most critical part of getting out of the bottom is to get as "mad as hell" about being there. That's right! You must get mad at it to beat it. Passion and tenacity must be in unison as you claw your way back to the top. Save the smiles for later when you are in the pit of despair. Grit your teeth and focus, focus, focus! Direct all energy into positive, productive tasks only. No excuses!

Remember that faith, confidence, and determination anchor your vision. The great resolve built by these three will help you "outlast your obstacle". The greater your challenge the greater your future. The lessons from knowing rock bottom will build your character as you will "get up" and move to higher ground.

Dig in your spikes; fight with passion and your clients will pull you out!

9

Theme: Dealing with pressure

Pressure!

"O Lord, will you keep in perfect peace him
whose mind is steadfast because he trusts in you.
Trust in the Lord forever, for the Lord,
the Lord, is the Rock eternal."
-Isaiah 26:3-4

Years and years of pressure make a fine diamond! The size of the diamond is not the only characteristic that makes her valuable. The cut and flawlessness aids in giving a small diamond sparkle and fire! Pressure is a major ingredient in winning. The hotter the oven, the faster your dough will rise! Pressure has many symptoms that we all know well. The most common are fluttering butterflies, cramps, headaches, or upset stomachs. Pressure is a complex feeling that you need help controlling. Pressure can be contained alone; however, we can also keep it in check with our value added support team. The company that you keep plays a large part in your ability to handle pressure. Remember not all of your clients like you and are in your corner. Successful professional, beware!

Clients that have hidden agendas can transport extreme mental fatigue on to you. Remember that no matter what challenges come your way, you have your faith that anchors you. The Lord will dispatch angels to help you handle those tough situations. One of the best ways to control pressure begins with rehearsal. I remember working on a very large customer opportunity in Winston-Salem. The opportunity was for a significant purchase of Industrial Supply products. The competitors came from all over the place as this was a once in a lifetime opportunity.

I can recall sitting in that conference room with my hands becoming damp with perspiration for the first time in my life. The size of the conference room table was also a bit intimidating as it would seat twenty people comfortably. The monarch butterflies were dancing around that day in my stomach. The only thing I had on my side was a very dynamic manager named Thomas. My manager was one of those guys who lives on pressure and welcomes danger! We prepared and rehearsed our proposal for this particular opportunity for an entire month. We role played rebuttals from the client and competitors that would be in that room. Thomas constantly reminded me of the next two ingredients in handling pressure, which are refinement and polish. The meeting began at about 9:00 so Thomas and I refined our presentation at 7:30 and again at 8:30. Thomas was excellent when it came to closing large opportunities because of the intense preparation and refinement. What I learned that day was that you can read your competition. Thomas of course was sitting back like Jaws the killer white shark waiting for our competition to make a mistake in the meeting. Just like clockwork, our competition opened their presentation discussing price! Thomas is one of the great life coaches who always had excellent strategy on defense. Our strategy was on value! Thomas said to me after that meeting, "If we win this opportunity it is because we are boardroom pressure tested!" The fact that we refined our proposal and charged in with a polished delivery gave us an advantage.

Our competitors were on their heels as they asked many questions during the meeting; we, on the other hand, delivered solution after solution. We overcame the pressure in the room because we were "prepared!" So, how did Thomas and I fare in the outcome? We "won" the opportunity! I am so thankful to Tom for the mentorship, tutelage and sponsorship of my strengths and abilities. He taught me to never give in to the pressure but to rehearse, refine, polish and deliver a world class presentation!

Successful professional, when you feel pressure do not run and hide; instead, batten down the hatch and go to war.

Here are my top tips for handling pressure:

> **Rehearse:**
> Prepare for every scenario and role play the dialogue.
> Give your spouse a presentation on what you are up against.
> Give your value added support team a call. Talk it through with them.
> Pray for the outcome that you want! Dream your victory up!

> **Refine:**
> Remove unneeded jargon and shorten your message.
> Inject action and confidence words in your vocabulary like "collaboration" and "partnership."
> Remove distractions that may impede your critical thinking.
> Keep your solution as simple as possible.

> **Polish:**
> No matter what challenge you are pressured with, handle it with class.
> Remember to have good sportsmanship. Win graciously and if you lose; lose in fun.

> **Deliver:**
> Remember, when you are under pressure, always under promise and over deliver.
> Smile! The customer wants you to win.
> Deliver the results on time and have all of the action items completed.
> Successful professional, you are a person of your word so let your yes mean yes and your no mean no.

Successful professional, you have what it takes to win against pressure. Pressure is a sign that you need to get prepared about something! So when you feel it coming your way, pray for power, rally your troops and **RRPD**!

Rehearse, Refine, Polish and Deliver.

The butterflies are coming.

"Don't be scared of presentations! Just think the people are stuffed animals. Yup! They're just little bitty puppy dogs!"
-My son, Harrison Tate Mckinley Goode (7 years old)

I just love my children! My daughter Kennedy was eight years old and preparing to give her first speech. Kennedy was running for secretary of Kimmel Farms Elementary School. Kennedy had been wrestling all night about the speech that she would have to give to about 120 of her classmates. I have to admit my heartbeat had picked up a bit as I thought about her calm personality. The nervousness came to a head the morning before the speech as we prepared a big breakfast for Kennedy. I thought everything was fine, but then she said "Daddy, I think I have some butterflies in my stomach!" I said "Yup! You have them alright and they are good for you. They let you know that you are alive and you are getting ready to receive a special reward." What was so special about that morning was that Kennedy received some special uplift from an unexpected source: her little brother, Harrison! As we traveled to school that morning Harrison was determined to get his big sister elected and immediately started to pump her up. Harrison, who was seven, said "Daddy; put on 'Pump It' by the Black Eyed Peas!" Suddenly, out of nowhere, Harrison made an analogy to his sister that floored me. It went "Ken; just think of all the students in the entire school as stuffed animals." It floored me. Kennedy busted out laughing and said "Brother you are right. I'm not scared of those puppy dogs." Kennedy went on and gave her speech and by 3:00 pm she was the third grade secretary of her elementary school.

Successful professional, we are all like Kennedy when it comes to butterflies. The butterflies in your stomach are signs that you are ready to hit a home run! Butterflies signal to us that we are happy, nervous, fearful, prepared or confident about a goal. You control your butterflies by looking back over your past wins and accomplishments. Yeah! You have to brag on yourself sometimes. If you do not think you have it in you then no one else will either. Successful professional, the butterflies that we experience aid in our decision making and we must take the time to acknowledge them. The nervousness that we feel helps with our timing. Life has rhythm to it and you must be on beat if you want to hit a home run. Timing is a key element in unlocking your productivity. Your journey to new endeavors will be very strange and you will be unsure of your footing. The butterflies will present themselves and your internal emotions will take over; it will be at that moment when timing is of the essence. Successful professional, take your calculated risks and enjoy the butterflies. The more you allow your butterflies to roam inside you the better your timing will be to close the opportunity. Don't be scared of those opportunities; they are just little bitty stuffed animals. Ha, ha…

You do not want to contain all of your butterflies.
Open the lid and let some of them go!

Have some fun! Hit a home run!

Decisions, decisions.

"The steps toward greatness involve making the right choices.
However, the choice means nothing if you
do not make the right decision."
-Antwain T. Goode

Unlocking your full repertoire of talents and abilities requires discipline and good decision making! Your relentless pursuit of achievement must not be jeopardized by the poor decisions of others. My mother always says "You are judged by the company that you keep" and of course she is right. The people with whom we associate ourselves have influence on some of our decisions. Successful professional, guard your dreams and aspirations as though they were gold. Make the right decision to share them with the people who can make them a reality. The choices that we make echo through the fabric of our lives, but the decisions from those choices can make or break future generations. Clients want people who are decisive and can execute. The buzzword that you will need to strengthen your decision making is "confidence". OK. Successful professional, it is time to take off the boxing gloves. The training that you have built from every chapter in this book will enable you to move toward your goal with purpose.

Champ, let's go into the confidence gym. The first hour of gym training begins with hitting the naysayer punching bag. Punch this bag relentlessly! You must believe that the course that you chart is the right one no matter what others say. Never forget it is your million dollars on the line. The next exercise to build confidence is skipping rope (timing). Successful professional, timing plays a critical role in capturing an opportunity. Timing is the right person, in the right place, at the right time, doing the right thing. Keeping your finger on the pulse of your life and knowing when to move will give you balance needed for those unanticipated challenges. Now it is time to hit the speed bag (tasks). The tasks that you need to complete must be hit rapidly one by one. Do not squander time when it comes to making a decision. Develop a scenario planning mindset. Successful professional, you must anticipate possible outcomes for the decision you are about to make. Scenario planning will peel back the layers of complex decisions and enable you to use your value added support team to help you.

Finally, get into the ring. Yes! It is time to fight. Confidence comes from going into the battle. The success that you will attain will be equal to the sweat equity you exhibit in the ring. You have been in training throughout this book and have developed new skill sets, so use them in your decision making. The hardest decision to make is not making one. You have all of the tools to win so be "confident" and win. Ding! Winner and still heavy weight champion in the world: "YOU!"

Here are my top confidence builders that will help you in your decision making:

> **Touch your weak areas.**
  (Be honest with yourself about where you need to apply resources in your life and get it done.)
  Do not harp on your shortcomings. Just touching them once in a while will increase your current strengths.

> **Win a small battle.**
  (Before fighting the number one heavy weight contender, knock out a small opponent.)
  Small victories will give you the confidence to win the main event!

> **Have a party.**
  (Celebrate decisions that create wins for you or others.) Enjoy the fruits of a good decision!

> **Get your advanced degree.**
  (Your professors will strengthen your mind in ways you have never imagined!)

➤ **Take a trip out of the country.**
(Broaden your horizons by understanding other cultures. When you get back home you will make better decisions on how you are spending your time.)

➤ **Get a prayer partner.**
(A prayer partner will help you stay focused on your spirituality and faith!) The more you pray the more the Lord will stretch your confidence and help you develop someone else. Prayer partners prop you up and push you forward.

➤ **Geronimo!**
(On some decisions in life you just have to take a chance!) Take the leap of faith. You will never know much faith you have until you jump off the cliff.

➤ **You have a parachute!**
(God will always be there with you!) If you make a decision that just does not work do not panic.
Remember this scripture:
"The Lord is my light and my salvation- whom shall I fear?"
Psalm 27:1

➤ **Love.**
(Love conquers all.) Decisions sometime require us to dig deep within ourselves, so allow love to be a hero and save the day.

Successful professional, when it comes to decisions remember the secret weapon.

Confidence, confidence, confidence!

Apply your resources. Get some help!

"A road trip is always better when you have
a co-pilot to stay awake with you."
-Antwain T. Goode

Leadership lives in all of us but it must be unleashed. We hear the complaint throughout organizations that leadership is missing on many cross functional teams. People who possess strong leadership characteristics did not achieve them overnight. The behavior patterns that they have chosen have formed incredible mental patterns of achievement. Successful professional, you are an overachiever and have greatness inside of you! Leadership arises from multiple successful completed tasks. The more you do something, the better you get. The better you get, the easier it will be to replicate that performance.

A critical step in leadership is your visibility! You must showcase your talents and skills on select tasks. In order to be considered a leader you must be available and ambitious. Everyone you meet is a gift from God and each person is armed with incredible abilities. In order to benefit from the merging of ideas and shared resources you must be thought of as an upright person. People are often obligated to rally to solve a challenge if they work for the same organization or team. Keep in mind that just because you are working for the same organization or team does not mean that people want to work with you! In order to lead you must show yourself as a friendly person and a person who cares.

Now that we have level set leadership, let's put it to use by raising our hands and asking for help. Help is wonderful; do not think of asking for help as a sign of weakness. Help rallies, inspires and promotes! Help is a key component in networking. Leaders are made stronger by asking for new ideas and introducing new mediums for collaboration. Successful professional, do not limit your circle of friends and acquaintances. Because of your unleashing of leadership you will be sought out through the grapevine and offered unique networking avenues. The footprint of your leadership will be that of friendship, loyalty and integrity. So, go ahead and choose a co-pilot or squadron for your next mission.

You have infectious leadership so be bold and assertive as you surround yourself with powerful allies who will guard your blind spots and give you better peripheral vision.

Get "help" and choose your "help" wisely!

Remember: no regrets! Your dreams are at your grasp.

Grab them!

If you can breathe, you have an opportunity to seize your dreams and shock the world! Successful professional, everything that you have learned in this book will be an asset to your brand. The brand recognition that you will market will be passed on to the people that you meet, your family, friends and future generations. My book says "yes" to you! The belief that you have in yourself is what makes everything go. Everyone sees your talents and abilities but it is up to you to fully unlock all of your unlimited capabilities. The unleashing of your new brand will give you global reach. You will build a spider web of new relationship networks. The excitement and momentum that you have built by writing your mission statement will anchor your dreams and take you to uncharted areas of your mind. Successful professional, you will be more productive and ignite the productivity in others.

I hope that the tools in *Bet the Farm* have unlocked some untapped talents and abilities that have been in hibernation. The goals that you have are attainable if you believe in yourself, your mission statement and your value added support team. You are more capable than ever before, so use this guide as a building block to grasp your dreams today! The courage to write this book stemmed from countless hours of prayer, determination and persistence. The organizations or clients that you serve want you and need the value that you bring to the table. You are now unleashed so blow away the competition. You have nothing to lose. Roll up your sleeves, dig in your spikes and set your sights to the hills from which cometh you help, and…

Bet The Farm!

Author's Final Thoughts

Bet the Farm will be an asset to someone who wants move toward their dreams but are missing a few key points on how to get there. Unlocking the productivity inside of you will open up many new doors and enable you to execute your plan. Have no fear in aiming for your dreams! Dreams do not just explode into our heads for any reason; they are God-breathed into us and because of that, they are meant to come to fruition. Know that you are a tool in God's tool box, so allow him to use you. Stay confident, stay determined, and be bold. I would love to hear from you! To contact me, write to:

Dr. Antwain Tate Goode
P.O Box 30231
Winston-Salem, NC. 27130

Be more prepared today to reach your dreams!

Unleash the productivity within you.

Bet The Farm!

Go for it all.

Edwards Brothers Malloy
Thorofare, NJ USA
November 11, 2015